SHE RETIRED
HAPPILY
EVER AFTER

TERESA BEAR
& BONNIE SWANSON
ILLUSTRATIONS BY JAMES BEAR

SHE RETIRED HAPPILY EVER AFTER

HOW TO MAKE YOUR FINANCIAL DREAMS COME TRUE

Copyright © 2012 by Teresa Bear

All rights reserved. No part of this book may be used or reproduced in any manner whatsoever without prior written consent of the author, except as provided by the United States of America copyright law.

Published by Advantage, Charleston, South Carolina.
Member of Advantage Media Group.

ADVANTAGE is a registered trademark and the Advantage colophon is a trademark of Advantage Media Group, Inc.

Printed in the United States of America.

ISBN: 978-159932-318-3
LCCN: 2012945466

This publication is designed to provide accurate and authoritative information in regard to the subject matter covered. It is sold with the understanding that the publisher is not engaged in rendering legal, accounting, or other professional services. If legal advice or other expert assistance is required, the services of a competent professional person should be sought.

Advantage Media Group is proud to be a part of the Tree Neutral® program. Tree Neutral offsets the number of trees consumed in the production and printing of this book by taking proactive steps such as planting trees in direct proportion to the number of trees used to print books. To learn more about Tree Neutral, please visit www.treeneutral.com. To learn more about Advantage's commitment to being a responsible steward of the environment, please visit www.advantagefamily.com/green

Advantage Media Group is a leading publisher of business, motivation, and self-help authors. Do you have a manuscript or book idea that you would like to have considered for publication? Please visit www.advantagefamily.com or call **1.866.775.1696**

This book is dedicated to my husband and handsome prince,
Desert Little Bear.

The author's legal counsel recommends the inclusion of the following information. Reading this section may cause drowsiness. Do not study it while driving a motor vehicle or operating heavy machinery. Mixing the text with alcohol will increase the fatigue's severity. Reading it numerous times in succession may induce paralysis, coma, or, in extreme cases, death from boredom. This section is best studied under the influence of espresso, Red Bull, Mountain Dew or other highly caffeinated beverages. It is also best studied if concerns about your investment portfolio keep you awake at night (see Appendix A).

DULL LEGAL SECTION

This book is designed to provide accurate and authoritative information regarding retirement planning and personal finances. It is meant to educate and inform the reader about general investment vehicles, concepts, and strategies. Neither the author nor the publisher is engaged in providing accounting, legal, investment, or other professional services through the publication of this book. The reader is encouraged to seek competent, professional representation for his or her personal financial, tax, and legal situation. The author and the publisher will not be responsible for any liability, loss, or risk resulting from the use and/or application of the information contained in this book. Examples used herein are for illustrative purposes only and are not intended to project the performance of any specific investment.
The information and sources named in the book and the Internet resources referenced therein were correct at the time of the publi-

cation. However, neither the author nor the publisher can assume responsibility for website changes made subsequent to publication.

KIND READERS

No one is perfect. I am thankful for the many people who have reviewed this book prior to publication. However, I recognize that being human means mistakes can be (and, in this case, probably were) made. As Alexander Pope wrote, "To err is human; to forgive, divine."[1] Gentle readers, I beg your forgiveness and understanding in advance. It is my hope perfection will come with the second edition.

Investment Advisory Services are offered through Brookstone Capital Management, LLC. Brookstone Capital Management, LLC, is not affiliated with JC Grason, LLC, of Mesa.

The Certified Financial Planner Board of Standards, Inc., owns the certification marks CFP®, CERTIFIED FINANCIAL PLANNER™, and federally registered CFP (with flame design) in the U.S., which it awards to individuals who successfully complete the CFP Board's initial and ongoing certification requirements.

A note before you begin this story:

If you are searching for a handsome prince to ride to your rescue on a fast white steed (or maybe in a flashy red convertible) and take care of you for the rest of your life, you are in the wrong place. Stop reading right now! Close the book immediately!

You're still reading, so I guess you don't need a handsome prince. How about a fairy godmother?

While there's no fairy godmother in this book, turn the page and I'll introduce you to the next best thing: your "fairy Godvisor," Teresa Bear, and some of her helpers.

About the Author

Teresa Bear specializes in retirement planning and asset preservation for retirees and their loved ones. Teresa is the President of JC Grason, LLC, Mesa, which is located in the Phoenix area.

Do you remember how the fairy godmother helped Cinderella pursue her dreams? Teresa does the same for her clients. Many women have the type of financial plan that contains a jumbled mix of CDs, stocks, bonds, mutual funds, and annuities. Teresa strives to transform these assets into beautiful financial plans that perfectly fit each client's individual needs, whether those needs include ensuring lifetime income, protecting against unnecessary taxation, insuring against disability, or creating a legacy (either for family members or a beloved charity). She specializes in creating the best plan to meet each client's fondest dreams. However, unlike the transformations in Cinderella, Teresa's plans aren't magic and don't expire at the stroke of midnight. Instead, they are in place as permanent foundations for financial protection, providing freedom from worry.

Teresa, a graduate of Iowa's Graceland University, has an MBA from the University of Kansas. She is a certified public accountant who has been practicing in the area of taxation for over twenty-five years. Additionally, she is a CERTIFIED FINANCIAL PLANNER™ who combines her knowledge of taxes with her expertise in investments.

Teresa searched for a handsome prince for many years. She was about to give up when she met Desert Little Bear, a Native American artist and a member of the Pasqua Yaqui tribe. His artwork is unique. He specializes in creating rock art (petroglyphs) using Arizonan natural stone. Desert's artistic genes have been passed on to his and Teresa's only son, James, who created the amazing illustrations for this book.

About the Contributing Author

Bonnie M. Swanson, JD, received her bachelor's degree from Pacific Lutheran University and her juris doctorate from Seattle University Law School. She has been licensed to practice law in Washington since 1990.

Bonnie has a wealth of experience in business law and tax. Her tax experience includes employment at Boeing's Corporate Tax Department, Deloitte & Touche, and Moss Adams, LLP. In addition to her background in tax, Bonnie has worked in commercial real estate development and is one of the founding members of a commercial real estate consulting and Internet marketing company.

In Washington, Bonnie's business law practice has included real estate, corporate and creditor representation. In addition, she has facilitated complex, multimillion-dollar asset sales and Chapter 11 reorganizations.

Her expertise in the world of business brokerage was sought out by *Phoenix Woman* magazine, to which she contributed two articles: "Close the Deal: 7 Steps to Selling Your Small Business"[2] and "Changing Hands: Know When and How to Sell Your Business."[3]

About the Illustrator

James Bear is an artistic prodigy who started drawing almost before he could walk. He is currently a senior at the New School for Arts and Academics in Tempe, Arizona.

At thirteen, James began his career as an award-winning professional artist, selling his work at art shows. He creates pieces in a variety of media: pen and ink, charcoal, ceramics, paint, and even Sharpie™ markers. His passion, however, is digital design. He began experimenting with digital art when he was only five years old and is pursuing a career in digital artwork and animation. James anticipates continuing his formal education at Arizona State University—and then, watch out, world!

She Retired Happily Ever After is James' first book.

Contents

Introduction 17

Chapter 1 23
    U.S. Taxpayers: Squeezed and Sent to the Juicing Room

Chapter 2 33
    The Three Stages of Nest-Egg Building

Chapter 3 43
    Who Will Help the Retiree Out?

Chapter 4 55
    History Repeats Itself Again and Again

Chapter 5 71
    The Many Flavors of Investments

Chapter 6 81
    The Naked Truth About Annuities

Chapter 7 97
    The Quest for the Perfect Investment

Chapter 8 115
    Building a Brick (Income) House

Chapter 9 127
    Playing "Keep Away" From Uncle Sam

Chapter 10 139
    Building a Solid Legal Foundation

Chapter 11 149
    Finding a "Real Advisor"

Appendix A: Determining Your Sleep Factor 157
Appendix B: Glossary 167
Endnotes 175

Introduction

Once Upon a Time...

It was the wedding of the century.

The blue sapphire and diamond engagement ring was on the finger of a young and beautiful woman. She was to be a princess, married to the heir to the throne. It was every girl's dream come true. Someday, she would be queen!

Her wedding gown was the palace's best-kept secret. Feverish speculation about the gown kept fashion experts guessing prior to the ceremony. Everyone was surprised and no one was disappointed. The bride was radiant in the custom-made gown: the handmade lace adorning the dress was as beautiful as the princess herself. Few brides get to "borrow" Cartier tiaras to top their veils, but the queen had lent this bride hers for the occasion.

An invitation to the royal wedding was the hottest ticket in town. VIPs from all over the world arrived for the event. Thousands of excited well-wishers camped out on the streets of London, hoping to get a glimpse of the happy couple. Millions of sparkling eyes were glued to television sets worldwide as the two recited their vows. When Charles and Diana were pronounced husband and wife, everybody watching knew that the couple would live happily ever after.

"SHE MARRIED THE HANDSOME PRINCE AND LIVED HAPPILY EVER AFTER."

Like many little girls, I grew up listening to fairy tales. The combination of innocent heroines, evil villains, witches, fairies, and magic cast a powerful spell over my imagination. In many of these stories, one consistent theme emerges over and over again: marrying the rich, handsome prince saves the beautiful, virtuous heroine from a horrible existence. Reading these stories, we learn that saying "I do" to the right guy solves all of our problems for the rest of our lives. However, as a grown-up, I have found that real life is more complicated. As I watched the dream of Diana and Charles' story turn into a nightmare, it became increasingly apparent that storybook weddings are not the same as storybook marriages.

Some lucky women find and marry handsome princes who love, honor, and cherish them during their entire lives. However, in reality, most women aren't so fortunate. In fact, "90 percent of all women will be solely responsible for their finances at some point in their lives."[4] This book is for that 90 percent!

Your Fairy Godvisor Says...

No matter what your current marital status is, remember that a man is not a financial plan!

Whether you're single, divorced, widowed, or happily married, this book has been designed with you in mind. Women have unique needs in retirement that often are not attended to by most financial planners. The bad news is that we can't rely on men to take care of us. The good news is that we can take care of ourselves!

According to a recent survey, more than half of all women are eager to learn more about money and investing. However, the difficulty of deciphering financial information is a critical barrier for many women.

When asked about their financial planning concerns, the women who participated in the survey responded as follows:

1. 44 percent thought the financial information was overwhelming, there was too much of it, or it was too hard to sort through.
2. 36 percent believed the information was complicated or hard to understand.
3. 32 percent found the available materials boring and dry.
4. 26 percent didn't understand the terminology, as if it were written in a foreign language.[5]

Having spent most of my career in the financial realm, I couldn't agree more with these sentiments! Even though I understand the lingo, most business books that I have read are boring. I wanted this book to be different.

Great teachers have always used stories to illustrate concepts their listeners found important. Aesop, a slave who lived in ancient Greece, created fables—many involving animals—to illustrate moral concepts. Past and present spiritual leaders have used and still rely on parables to reveal religious teachings. Overall, civilizations rely on stories to educate—from the Inuit people in the frozen north to the aboriginal tribes of the hot Australian outback.

One tale had a big impact on me when I was growing up. My first memory of this story dates to when I was five years old, when my family only had a black-and-white television. My father happened to work at a TV station and one Sunday evening he drove the whole family over to the station's transmitter in order to watch a movie.

I remember lying on the floor, curled up in blankets, mesmerized by the images on the screen. From the moment the drab, dull door of a farmhouse opened to a bright, beautiful world of flowers, revealing a pristine city and a bright yellow-brick road, I was entranced.

As a girl who grew up in Kansas, *The Wizard of Oz* has always had a special place in my heart. The story has many messages, and one of the most significant is empowerment. As Dorothy watches the Wizard float away in a balloon, she is heartbroken. Her dreams of returning home to Kansas have been shattered, and she believes she will never reach her destination. However, her final rescue comes from within herself. When Glinda arrives on the platform, she says, "You've always had the power to go back."[6] Ultimately, Dorothy helped herself.

Just as Glinda helped Dorothy to recognize the power within herself, my wish is to help my readers find that power within themselves. As you read this book, you will be educated about some very important retirement risks and strategies. Most women are more financially savvy than they give themselves credit for. After all, unless we have married princes, we often have to stretch limited dollars in order to care for our loved ones and ourselves. We know how to spend money wisely. However, even as we are infinitely capable of managing the money we spend, we are often woefully uneducated about how to manage the money we invest. Society tells us that men are more competent than women when it comes to managing the family investments. This is as much nonsense as the idea that men are incapable of nurturing a child (or changing a diaper). Just ask my husband!

INTRODUCTION

Drawing on the rich storytelling heritage of fairy tales, I use stories from my childhood to teach investment concepts (such as risk, tax, and income planning strategies). This book is designed to address both novice and experienced investors. It's my goal to educate you so that you, too, will be able to retire happily ever after!

CHAPTER 1

U.S. TAXPAYERS
SQUEEZED AND SENT TO THE JUICING ROOM

Once Upon A Time...

"Don't!" said Mr. Wonka.

"Fabulous!" shouted Violet. "It's tomato soup! It's hot and creamy and delicious! I can feel it running down my throat!"

"Stop!" said Mr. Wonka. "The gum isn't ready yet! It's not right!"

"It's changing!" shouted Violet, chewing and grinning both at the same time. "The second course is coming up! It's roast beef! It's tender and juicy! Oh boy, what a flavor! The baked potato is marvelous, too! It's got a crispy skin and it's all filled with butter inside!"

Mr. Wonka was waving his hands and saying, "No, no, no, no, no! It isn't right for eating! It isn't right! You mustn't do it!"

"Blueberry pie and ice cream!" shouted Violet. "Here it comes! Oh my, it's perfect! It's beautiful! It's ... it's exactly as though I'm swallowing it! It's as though I'm chewing and swallowing great big spoonfuls of the most marvelous blueberry pie in the world!"

"Good heavens, girl!" shrieked Mrs. Beauregarde suddenly, staring at Violet, "what's happening to your nose!"

"It's turning blue! Your nose is turning as blue as a blueberry!"

> "Your cheeks!" screamed Mrs. Beauregarde. "They're turning blue as well! So is your chin! Your whole face is turning blue!"
>
> "I told you I hadn't got it quite right," sighed Mr. Wonka, shaking his head sadly.
>
> But there was no saving her now. Her body was swelling up and changing shape at such a rate that within a minute it had turned into nothing less than an enormous round blue ball—a gigantic blueberry, in fact—and all that remained of Violet Beauregarde herself was a tiny pair of legs and a tiny pair of arms sticking out of the great round fruit and a little head on top.
>
> "It always happens like that," sighed Mr. Wonka ...

Excerpt from *Charlie and the Chocolate Factory* by Roald Dahl[7]

In *Charlie and the Chocolate Factory*, Violet Beauregarde is obsessed with bubble gum. She can't resist the promise of a tasty, three-course dinner inside in a single stick of gum. When she starts chewing, there isn't a big problem. However, as she continues chewing, disaster strikes.

What happened to Violet is similar to what has been happening to our national debt over the past few years.

As we review the U.S. debt crisis, let's look at one of the scariest Halloween costumes I've ever seen.

"I'm already $47,782 in debt and I only own a dollhouse."

Did you know that since September 28, 2007, our national debt has increased, on average, almost $4 billion (yes, that's "billion" with a "b") per day, every day?[8] Can you believe that? It's unfathomable.

As of this writing, the U.S. national debt was $15,076,727,706,197[9] and still increasing. That's 15 trillion dollars! Now, as a money-oriented person, I can wrap my head around what a million dollars is. I can even, somewhat, comprehend a billion dollars. However, as the numbers get bigger, even my eyes start to glaze over. Just 1 trillion dollars, let alone 15 trillion, is a whole lot of money!

The biggest problem is how quickly the numbers have increased, just over the past few years.

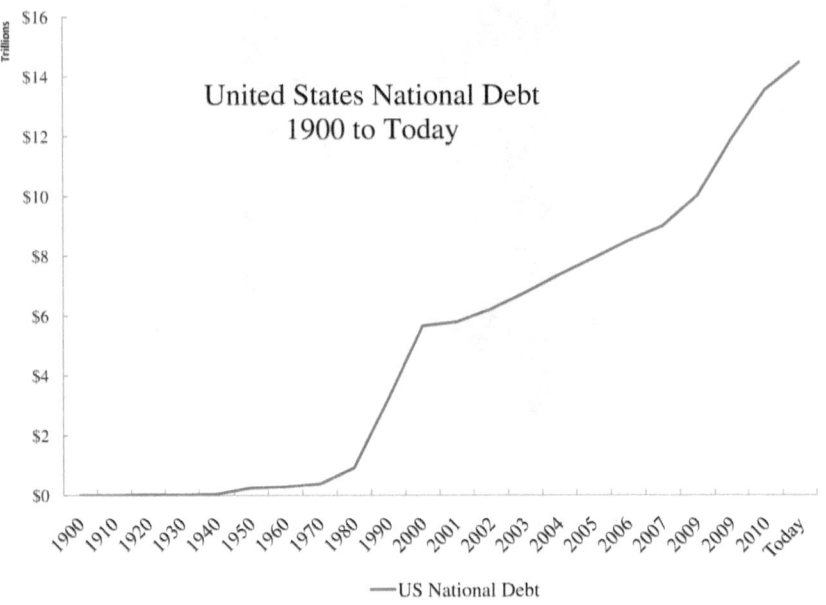

This chart shows the national debt's growth from 1900 to today[10]

Remember the year 1976? As a national group, we celebrated the United States' bicentennial with parades, speeches, and fireworks. We should have also celebrated our frugality. That year, the national debt was less than $700 million. Our national debt grew steadily during the next twenty-five years, and when the clocks struck midnight on December 31, 1999, the debt was about $5.6 trillion.

As of today, that number has almost tripled. This means that during the last eleven years, our government accumulated almost three times the debt that the United States had borrowed since John Hancock (and his fellows) signed the Declaration of Independence in 1776. Our founding fathers would be appalled. Like Violet in Willy Wonka's factory, Uncle Sam has been chewing the debt bubble gum. Now, he is a big, fat, bloated ball that might explode.

The Halloween costume was scary. Now, let's look at a website that is truly terrifying. This site, called USDebtClock.org, contains some of the most accurate, up-to-date information available about our country's financial condition. You'll see many mind-boggling statistics there, but I want to focus just on a couple of them.

A screenshot of USDebtClock.org on December 3, 2011[11]

First, let's take a look at the national debt. As mentioned above, it is now over $15 trillion. The national debt per citizen has increased to $48,209. However, as we saw in the picture of the little girl, that figure is the same whether you are a retired homeowner or a child with a dollhouse. If we dive in and look at the burden on actual taxpayers—that is, on you and me—we find that number increases nearly threefold, to $133,906.

Many retirees I work with are proud of the fact that they have retired debt-free. Credit cards, car loans, and mortgages are paid off. It's a measure of financial security. If you are one of those retirees, congratulations! You have worked hard and accomplished much. After all, younger generations of Americans embrace debt. Their spending and consumption habits mirror the U.S. federal government's uncontrolled spending.

Unfortunately, the U.S. federal government is now squandering your hard-earned retirement security. Even though your personal debts are paid off, as a taxpaying citizen you still have debts—courtesy of Uncle Sam—of over $133,000. If you are married, your joint debt is the astronomical sum of $266,000—over a quarter of a million dollars! Just when you thought you were financially set, you find you are responsible for a huge debt, which you're paying on behalf of a reckless government.

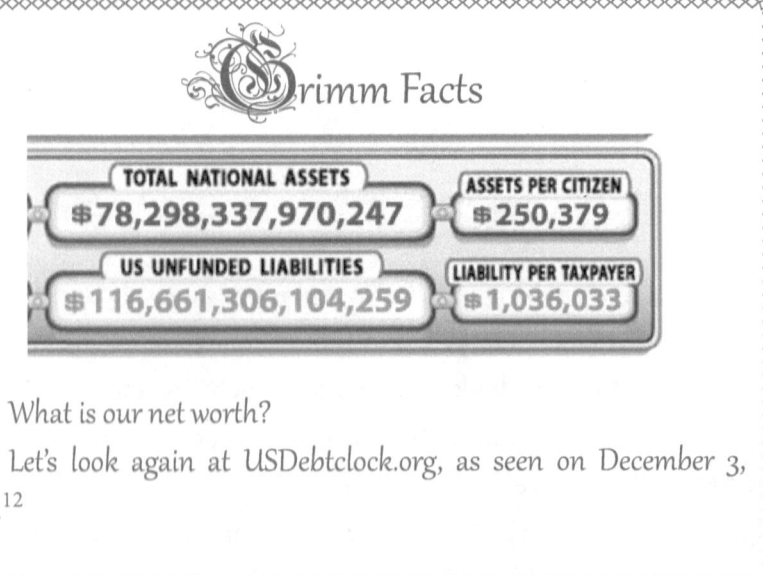

Grimm Facts

TOTAL NATIONAL ASSETS	ASSETS PER CITIZEN
$78,298,337,970,247	$250,379
US UNFUNDED LIABILITIES	**LIABILITY PER TAXPAYER**
$116,661,306,104,259	$1,036,033

What is our net worth?

Let's look again at USDebtclock.org, as seen on December 3, 2011.[12]

> If we also take a look at a couple more numbers from the same website—these numbers address what you and I would call net worth—we soon find that they don't look much better. Our total national assets amount to $78,298,337,970,247. This includes personal and business assets, as well as assets held by corporations and nonprofits.
>
> When we examine the liability side, the numbers are truly frightening. We have a projected future liability of $116,661,306,104,259 for programs such as Social Security, Medicare, and prescription drug coverage. That's 116 trillion dollars!

If we compare the assets to the liabilities, we find that each taxpayer has debts amounting to more than four times his or her share of national assets. Seeing the breakdown of these numbers per citizen is truly disturbing.

So, what happens to ordinary citizens (mere mortals, such as you and me) when our debts are greater than our assets? We declare bankruptcy, of course. Now, I am not saying our government is headed for bankruptcy or is going to default on its obligations, but our representatives in Washington have a big problem that desperately needs to be fixed.

What does that ballooning national debt mean for us today? How does it impact our everyday lives? Well, the biggest impact of the increasing debt has been its effect on the U.S. dollar. Just as the debt began exploding, the dollar began collapsing.

Chart created from data presented by the Board of Governors of the Federal Reserve System[13]

When Violet became a big, round blueberry, Willy Wonka sent her to the juicing room to be squeezed. Retirees have been squeezed as well. As the above chart shows, in just nine short years—since 2002—the dollar has lost a third of its value. So, every dollar you had in 2002 is now worth less than 68 cents!

Have your pension checks increased to make up for that 32 percent decrease? How about your Social Security checks? What about the value of your stocks? Has the interest on your CDs gone up since 2002? It's no wonder that the average retiree feels as if she has been sent to the juicing room.

Given these questions, what does the future hold? With all the government bailouts, the mountain of debt with which we're faced, and the general state of our economy, I believe a continued decline in the dollar is inevitable.

As discussed earlier, our country's debt (over $15 trillion) is at an all-time high. We are now citizens of the single most indebted nation in history, owing more to foreign investors, retirees, and ordinary citizens than we could ever hope to repay. To make matters worse, the first wave of baby boomers is now reaching retirement. This means unfunded government IOUs for Social Security, Medicare, and prescription drugs are coming due to the tune of an estimated $116 trillion.[14]

When we celebrated our bicentennial in 1976, the United States was the richest and most powerful nation in the world. Today, we are seeing China[15] and other foreign powers calling for a new reserve currency, seeking to move away from the U.S. dollar as the world's standard.

BUCKET FAMILY FINANCES

In *Charlie and the Chocolate Factory*,[16] Charlie Bucket's family is very poor. His father lost his job (screwing lids on toothpaste tubes) when the toothpaste factory closed. The family also has elder care issues, since all Charlie's grandparents are bedridden. While the Bucket family's finances aren't disclosed in the book, they might look a little something like this:

Bucket Family Total Annual Income	$21,740
Bucket Family Total Annual Spending	$38,190
Bucket Family New Credit Card Debt	$16,450
Bucket Family Credit Card Balance	$150,767

This would be a scary budget for any family. No wonder Charlie hopes he'll receive a golden ticket in his candy bar. It could have been the only way out. However, the above numbers are not just for the Buckets. If we remove 8 zeros from the 2011 federal budget[17] and the current national debt,[18] we see the United States' present financial predicament.

Do you think the U.S. government can find a golden ticket?

Chapter 2

The Three Stages of Nest-Egg Building

Once Upon A Time...

I worry about that son of mine. It's almost as if he got switched at birth. Don't get me wrong, I love him and appreciate the fact that he's stayed at the farm to help me out. Yet we are total and complete opposites. I've worked hard all my life—cooking, cleaning, sewing, and working the farm—trying to provide a secure home for my family. Safety is extremely important to me. But my son ... Well, Jack is a real gambler.

For instance, a few months ago we needed some money. So, I asked Jack to take our cow to town and sell it. Did he come home with cold, hard cash? No. He didn't. He met some slick salesman and traded that cow for some magic beans. I couldn't believe it when Jack came home and told me that story. "Mr. Slick" told him those magic beans were going to make us rich beyond our wildest dreams! Yeah, whatever. I'd heard that story before.

I couldn't take that nonsense. I was so furious that I just threw the beans out the window! Imagine the surprise and complete shock I felt when I saw the beans had grown into this huge beanstalk, which went so high into the sky I couldn't see the top. The thing almost looked like it dissolved in mid-air. I urged Jack to harvest some of the beans— thought it might provide a nice income. But that young guy bravado kicked in. Jack decided to climb the beanstalk and find out what was up there. I wanted him to be safe and stay on the ground, but he still believed that guy who had sold him the beans.

So, Jack climbed up and ended up putting his life in danger. There's some scary giant who lives at the top of the beanstalk and constantly yells, "Fe fi fo fum!" Jack told me that the giant tried to eat him. The giant is a cannibal!

Somehow, Jack managed to escape and came back with some gold coins. That really made a difference to our finances. But, then, because Jack is such a gambler, he went back up the beanstalk and grabbed a goose that lays golden eggs. Now we are really set: comfortable for life. We're financially secure; I just want to keep it that way. His gambles have finally paid off. I'm scared, though. Jack says he's going up the beanstalk again to try and find more treasure. I just don't understand it. I guess it's just a guy thing.

It's amazing how different a story can be when it's told from different perspectives. In "Jack and the Beanstalk," Jack's mother is never named—so I'll call just her Barbara. Barbara Beanstalk views her son's actions in a totally different light. When looking at this story from her perspective, as opposed to her son's, Jack's actions seem crazy.

Actually, there are some crazy differences between men and women and between different generations.

Your Fairy Godvisor Says...

If you don't happen to have a goose that lays golden eggs that can provide retirement income, your investment life is divided into three phases: accumulation, conservation, and distribution.

BUILDING YOUR NEST: THE ACCUMULATION PHASE

Think of the first stage of your investment life, the accumulation phase, as the time for building your nest egg. A bird begins building its nest by intricately weaving little bits of twigs and grass together until the construction is finally strong enough to support the mama bird and her chicks. This takes a great deal of time and work. Similarly, building your own retirement nest egg takes a great deal of time and work. We should start small, in our twenties or thirties, and begin building. It's really hard to get started; some young people think they can wait.

However, time is on your side when you are young and beginning early can make a huge difference in your future retirement. For instance if Jack started investing in stocks when he was twenty-five years old and wanted to retire forty years later, he could create a nest egg of over $500,000,[19] just by contributing $2,000 per year to an IRA. Like a bird that consistently weaves small twigs and grass into the nest until that nest is complete, you'll find that each small contribution to your nest egg makes a huge difference.

Grimm Facts

Not many people start young and consistently contribute to their retirement funds for forty years. According to a recent study, 54 percent of retirees have less than $25,000 in savings![20]

$25,000 is not a very big nest egg. It's more like a hummingbird's nest egg. I remember seeing a family of hummingbirds that built a nest in our roof ledge. It was about one inch in diameter, or about the size of a quarter. The nest was very tiny and cute. Yet while a tiny and cute hummingbird nest is fun to admire, no retiree wants a tiny, cute nest egg.

Retirees want eagle-sized nest eggs.

When I was growing up, my grandfather owned a ranch in Colorado. One day, as he was driving around the property, he discovered that a bald eagle had built her nest on a ledge overhanging a cliff. Even though the mama eagle felt nice and protected at the top of the cliff, Grandpa could drive right up to the mesa above her and look down at the babies. What an amazing sight! An eagle's nest, which often reaches over six feet in diameter, is a massive structure and an amazing feat of engineering.

An eagle's nest is no tiny hummingbird's nest that can be cupped in your hand—and crushed just as easily. An eagle uses big sticks to build her nest. Many times, each stick measures a full inch in diameter. She works for weeks carrying these sticks to the ledge and weaving them into a solid structure for her babies. Likewise, building a large nest egg can be hard, dangerous, and take lots of time and work.

PROTECTING YOUR NEST: THE CONSERVATION PHASE

The second stage of investing is the conservation phase. During this phase, you must ensure that you don't lose what you've worked so hard to build up.

When I was young, my family took me to visit that eagle's nest. I was able to stand above the nest and peer down at the babies. They were no more than six feet away. And boy, was that mama eagle mad when she spotted us. She did not like having us humans around one bit. She swooped down, like a dive-bomber in a dogfight as we looked at the babies. She was going to protect her nest at all costs.

Family photo of a baby eagle on a cliff in Colorado. Note my grandfather, kneeling just above the eaglet.

This is what retirees need to do with their nest eggs. Starting at around age fifty-five or sixty, retirees need to begin ensuring that their nests are protected with safe investments. This is not the time to take risks (that time was in your thirties and forties). This protecting-your-nest stage lasts from about age sixty to age eighty. In this stage, the major goal is to ensure that you have adequate income to last you the rest of your life.

FLEDGING: THE DISTRIBUTION PHASE

The final stage of building a nest is when the birds fledge and fly away, or the distribution phase. Unfortunately, I wasn't visiting my grandpa when those baby eagles fledged. However, Grandpa told me, and my family, about it. When a baby eagle is able to fly off the ledge and begin its new life, as an independent, free creature, the mama eagle's task is complete.

Similarly, retirees who have accumulated enough wealth for their own needs often want to see their own visions fly on. How is that type of legacy created? Whether you are thinking of children, grandchildren, or other family members—or maybe your religious institution or favorite charity—planning for this final stage is critical. Often, legacies have income tax consequences. For instance, if you are only taking minimum distributions out of an IRA, that IRA is a potential tax-related time bomb that will go off when you pass away. If planning isn't done correctly during the distribution stage, your income could be subject to double taxation when you pass away. The combined estate tax and income tax on IRAs can result in your least favorite uncle—Uncle Sam—being the biggest beneficiary of your IRA. Remember, if you don't plan for taxes, the IRS will.

For this stage of investing, proper planning means both tax and estate planning. It means working with trusted advisors in order to build a solid legal, tax, and investment foundation, ensuring that the eagle (your legacy) is able to soar.

THE BATTLE OF THE SEXES

Not only did Jack and Barbara Beanstalk have a generation gap that affected their views of investing, but they also had a sex-based difference in their approach to investing. An academic study comparing men and women's investment activities[21] confirmed what I have found in my experience working with clients: in general, men take more investment risks than women do. This might be biological, since men are more physically aggressive than women. Perhaps this biological difference also comes into play in terms of the amount of risk men and women take when investing. Possibly, women's need for safer investing comes from female programming to protect our homes and children. Security is vital for women's well-being.

Grimm Facts

The Allianz Women, Money, and Power Study found:

[...] a vast majority of women (90 percent) feel financially insecure, despite the fact they are more educated, more involved in financial decisions, and are controlling more of the wealth than ever before. Regardless of this level of insecurity, women said financial security and freedom are 15–20 times more important than money-related status and respect, with nearly two-thirds saying that the best thing about having money is feeling secure and not [having] the things money can buy.[22]

These sex-based differences in risk tolerance can affect retirees' portfolios in dramatic ways.

The need for low-risk investments hinders women's abilities to build large nest eggs during the accumulation stage. Because women often can't handle the volatility of investing in stocks, they take more conservative approaches. This can be disastrous, because women then lose the power of compound growth when building their nest eggs. For instance, if that $2,000 placed in an IRA only grows 4 percent annually (instead of 8 percent, as in the earlier example), after forty years, it is worth less than $200,000.[23] That's a difference of over $300,000.

The good news about this difference in risk tolerance is that what works against women during the accumulation phase works for them in the conservation and distribution phases (during their retirement years). Men who continue to invest aggressively risk losing everything they've worked for throughout their entire lives.

Women's natural tendency to protect those hard-earned dollars will allow them to keep the money they've earned and generate income for the rest of their lives. They will also be set up to pass assets on to their families—they will be able to see those baby birds fly away.

CHAPTER 3

WHO WILL HELP THE RETIREE OUT?

nce Upon a Time...

"Who will help me plant the seed?"

"Not I," grunted the greedy pig.

"Not I," purred the fat cat.

"Not I," squeaked the scheming rat.

"Well, then," the Little Red Hen said, "I will do it."

The Little Red Hen continued to ask all of her friends for assistance with the various chores involved in turning a seed into a loaf of bread.

"Who will help me harvest the wheat?"

"Who will help me thresh the wheat?"

"Who will help me take the wheat to the mill?"

"Who will help me bake the bread?"

Each time, her friends declined to help her. However, her friends had a little change of attitude when it was time for the Little Red Hen's final question.

"Who will help me eat the bread?"

"I will," meowed the cat.

> "I will," squeaked the rat.
>
> "I will," squealed the pig.
>
> They all stood in line to grab the fruits of her labor. However, in most versions of "The Little Red Hen" story, the hen doesn't feed the other lazy animals the bread she worked so hard to produce. Instead, she saves it for herself and her family.

Female retirees often feel as though they are in the same barnyard as the Little Red Hen. They have worked all of their lives to support themselves and their families, to create a comfortable living in their retirement. However, when that time comes, they find there are lots of greedy animals trying steal that hard-earned bread.

The rats of the government tax the retiree's hard-earned savings and diminish her Social Security checks. The fat cats on Wall Street churn her accounts for high commissions after failing to protect her assets when the markets crashed. The pigs at the bank are paying her next to nothing on her CDs, while happily accepting billions of dollars in bailout funds.

None of these animals were around when the retiree sacrificed to buy new shoes for her children—and none for herself. They weren't there when she got up at 6:00 a.m. to make breakfast for her family and ran nonstop all day until, at 11:00 p.m., she put the final dish away and stole fifteen minutes to relax in the bathtub before collapsing in bed.

GOVERNMENT RATS

Government rats are standing first in line to take retirees' hard-earned bread. Many women work two jobs: the paid one at the office, hospital, or factory, and the unpaid one at home. However, despite their faithful contributions to the Social Security System, women (as a group) are not receiving the same Social Security checks their male counterparts do.

One of the reasons for smaller checks is that women's work is undervalued in this society. Predominantly female professions pay less than those staffed by men. As studies also show, even when placed in the same job, women earn less than men do. The good news is that women's pay, in relationship to men's, has increased during the last thirty years (from 60.2 percent in 1980 to 77.4 percent in 2010).[24] The bad news is that we still are not even, and this wage disparity in the workplace has a dramatic effect on retirement.

Grimm Facts

In 2010, according to the Social Security Administration, the average annual Social Security income received by women sixty-five years and older was $11,794; for men, it was $15,231.[25]

My math shows that women's Social Security checks are 22 percent smaller than men's. In other words, we ladies are forced to live on about three-quarters of the income that men do.

To add insult to injury, the purchasing powers of those Social Security checks are not going up. As we discussed earlier, the dollar has decreased in value by 32 percent in the last nine years. Social Security checks have not kept up with this change. From 2002 to

2010, the total increases in Social Security checks to compensate for increases in the cost of living were only 24.3 percent; in 2010 and 2011, there were no Social Security inflation increases at all.[26] Some seniors witnessed a decrease in their net checks because their Medicare payments increased. To retirees, it feels like the sneaky government rats have been at it again, stealing from the seniors.

Finally, the income taxes women pay on their Social Security checks have continued to climb. Until 1984, Social Security benefits were not taxed. In 1984, "high income" recipients (people with annual incomes over $25,000 for single taxpayers and over $32,000 for married taxpayers) began paying taxes on a portion of their benefits. Those thresholds have not increased with inflation. To compound the problem, the potential portion of taxable benefits has increased from 50 percent to 85 percent. Congress members have even discussed making Social Security benefits 100 percent taxable.

THE FAT CATS OF WALL STREET

What is an average investor to do? Once upon a time, brokers bought blue-chip stocks for their clients, held those stocks for a long time, and sold them when the clients needed income. Those days are long gone.

Enter the Internet. Now, trades are placed twenty-four hours a day, seven days a week. Events overseas instantly impact markets in the United States. Day traders pay high rents to have their offices close to the computer banks on Wall Street. That way, their trades can be executed faster (and for better prices) than those of the mere mortals living in Anytown, USA.

Bernie Madoff, who was trusted by thousands of investors, was jailed for his crimes.

Some of the financial abuses are criminal. Bernie Madoff went to jail for 150 years to pay for his crimes: defrauding investors of an estimated $64.8 billion in what was the largest Ponzi scheme ever pulled off by an individual. The saddest thing about this scam was that there were lots of warning signs, all of which were ignored by the government and press watchdogs.

Although illegal schemes are terrible, most average investors are hurt every day by the big brokerage firms conducting business as usual. And it's all 100 percent legal.

The dirty little secret of Wall Street is how brokerage firms make their money. The general public is led to believe that the commissions brokerage firms pay their stockbrokers to execute trades and manage their accounts are what support these firms. This is only partially true. There are actually two sides to most Wall Street brokerage firms: the retail investor side (that's you and me) and the investment banking side.

The investment banking side makes huge profits for the firm. Most people have heard of the 80/20 rule: 80 percent of the profits are made by 20 percent of the customers. Who do you think the top customers are at the brokerage firms? They are the big, corporate customers who use the firms to raise their capital.

THE STORY OF THE TWO LITTLE COYOTES

Here's how it works. Let's say ACME Corporation wants to expand its operations in Arizona. They're building a theme park with such thrilling rides as the Crazy Cliff Plunge, the Roaring Rocket Launcher, and the Train in a Tunnel. ACME has been able to purchase land and its executives are positive that, "If they build it, people will come." ACME is sure that ACMELAND will be the family destination for the future, drawing roadrunners in their RVs from everywhere. To raise the $500,000,000 needed to build the park, ACME approaches the investment firm of Wylie and Wily.

This investment firm has two divisions. The Wylie division gets everything ready for ACME's rocket launch: preparation for the park. They put together the legal and regulatory paperwork, file documents with the government, and are paid the handsome sum of $25,000,000.

On the day the offering is made available to the public, the Wily division of the firm gets to work. Its brokers call all of their retail customers—again, that's people like you and me—and say something like this:

You are so lucky to be on the ground level of an opportunity of a lifetime. This could be the next Disneyland™. I'm calling you because you are one of my top clients. If you want, I think I can get you some of this stock. We don't know where the price will go after the initial offering, but this deal is as big as the Arizona desert. In fact, our firm's analysts have rated this a solid "buy." If you don't act on this now, I can't guarantee the future price.

Of course the firm's analysts have rated the deal a buy. Wylie and Wily's profits are dependent on the check ACME writes to fund the whole deal. Other firms on Wall Street likely want to earn ACME's business in the future and are hesitant to be pessimistic about the deal's prospects. So, ACME Corporation gets $475,000,000 to build the park, another $25,000,000 goes to Wylie and Wily, and everyone is happy. Right?

However, what if no one comes to ACMELAND, and the rocket comes plummeting to the earth? What if the stock becomes worthless? In that case, Acme Corporation still got $475,000,000, and Wylie and Wily still got $25,000,000; it's the investors who crashed.

The problem with the current system is that the average investor can't depend on her stockbroker to put her needs first. Brokers do not have a fiduciary duty to their clients.

WHAT'S THAT?

What is a fiduciary duty? The word *fiduciary* is derived from the Latin term *fiduciarius*, which means "holding in trust." It is a pledge.

I recall that when I was a small child in kindergarten, my school furnished me with a little bracelet made of beads to wear on my right wrist during morning assembly. Along with the other children, during each assembly, I was instructed to place my right hand over my chest and state, "I pledge allegiance to the flag …"

> ### Your Fairy Godvisor Says...
> *Investment advisor representatives take a pledge, but instead of pledging allegiance to the flag, they pledge allegiance to their clients. This is in stark contrast to stockbrokers. Believe it or not, a stockbroker's duty of trust is to his or her firm—not the clients. Stockbrokers have a suitability standard, which is a lower standard of care than that of fiduciary duty (see Appendix B).*

On July 21, 2010, in response to the crash of 2008, President Obama signed the Dodd–Frank Wall Street Reform and Consumer Protection Act into law. The 2,000-page bill was designed to increase regulatory oversight and prevent Wall Street abuses. However, despite urgings by consumer advocates, state regulators, the Certified Financial Planning Board, and other financial industry organizations,[27] the bill did not include uniform fiduciary standards for all investment advisors.[28]

For now, your stockbroker is not required to pledge his or her allegiance to you. A stockbroker's primary loyalty is to the brokerage firm he or she is working for.

BANK PIGS

The banks are—in my opinion—the worst of the bunch, and Charles Munger agrees. Munger has worked side by side with his partner, Warren Buffett, to build up their company, Berkshire Hathaway. In his remarks to investors at Berkshire Hathaway's annual shareholder meeting in 2011, Munger stated, "Investment bankers and mortgage issuers were afflicted with insanity, megalomania, and evil when they helped inflate the pre-2008 housing bubble."[29]

In their unrelenting quest for greed and profit, bank leaders put aside any semblance of rational thought and began loaning money, like crazy, to people who had no business buying homes, because they could not afford them. These loans—subprime mortgages—have always been around. In the early years of this century (2001–2003), the percentage of these loans held steady between 7 and 8 percent. However, during the next four years, that number increased almost threefold, to around 20 percent.[30]

"Easy credit" policies from the banks lead to a dramatic surge in the number of homebuyers. The increase in demand for homes then inflated housing prices. This, in turn, led to the housing bubble, which popped in 2007 and, ultimately, led to the banks' collapse on Wall Street and the financial meltdown in 2008. Trillions of dollars were lost in the housing meltdown and stock market crash, and much of that may never be recovered.

I reside in the Phoenix metro area, which was one of the hardest hit areas in the country. I have clients who invested in homes and lost thousands of dollars. A house purchased for $325,000 in 2007 might sell today for $125,000. Someday, prices may recover, but I doubt I will live long enough to see it.

Sadly, we, as taxpayers, have rescued the banks from their bad business decisions. The federal government has funneled over $432 billion[31] of bailout money into these banks to purchase or insure their "troubled assets."[32]

Grimm Facts

Because of the 2008 financial crisis, interest rates have plummeted. For retirees, who depend on income from their investments, this has been a disaster. In October 2008, retirees could find a six-month CD that paid 4.37 percent. Three years later, that rate plummeted to .5 percent.[33] In other words, in just three short years, our Little Red Hen has seen an 80 percent decrease in her CD interest income. Meanwhile, the banks haven't changed the interest rates they charge on credit card loans: the average is still about 14 percent.[34] Poor Little Red Hen must be a bit confused about this disparity.

So, we can conclude that since 2008 the banks have now potentially hurt our hard-working Little Red Hen in four ways:

1. The value of her house is down.

2. The value of her stock market investment portfolio is down.
3. The rate that she earns on her CDs is down.
4. The money used to fund the bailouts comes from her taxes, which may be higher for years.

After all those years of working hard for herself and her family, her income is snatched away by the government rats, the Wall Street fat cats, and the bank pigs. The Little Red Hen is left wondering if there will be any crumbs remaining of the bread she worked so hard to bake.

CHAPTER 4

HISTORY REPEATS ITSELF AGAIN AND AGAIN

Once Upon a Time...

Jack and Jill went up the hill
To fetch a pail of water.
Jack fell down and broke his crown,
And Jill came tumbling after.

Doesn't the story of Jack and Jill seem like it also describes the way the stock market behaves? We plod up the hill and, just as we reach the top, some crisis happens and we fall down—and hurt ourselves. The one certainty about the stock market is that it will go up—and down. The big uncertainty lies in how high it goes and how low it falls ... and when that plunge is going to happen.

The second verse of "Jack and Jill" goes like this:

Up Jack got, and home did trot,
As fast as he could caper,
To old Dame Dob, who patched his nob
With vinegar and brown paper.

I have to admit that before writing this book I was unaware of the medicinal properties of vinegar and brown paper: maybe one of my readers can enlighten me on this. It's comforting to know that neither child was seriously hurt; the next day, Dame Dob probably sent them up the hill again.

However, picture this in your mind: Jack and Jill are no longer seven—they are seventy. How does that fall down the hill change as we get older? Well, just as physical falls become far more painful and serious as we age, falls in our investments' value are more serious during retirement.

Do you believe that history repeats itself?

Do you believe that market history repeats itself?

Let's take a little nostalgic walk back through time.

"IT WAS THE BEST OF TIMES; IT WAS THE WORST OF TIMES": 1924 TO 1944

The Great War was over. After the unspeakable horrors, it was time to party. The new sounds of jazz were being played in nightclubs. Times were good. Women showed their legs and bobbed their hair. In the United States they voted for the first time.

During the Roaring Twenties, America was on the move. Automobiles were mass-produced. By 1927 Henry Ford had sold 15 million Model T Fords. That same year, Charles "Lucky Lindy" Lindbergh crossed the Atlantic Ocean, ushering in the potential for commercial aviation.

Innovation was everywhere. "Talkies" had replaced the silent films of earlier times, and entire communities were entertained in movie houses.

Then, after a period of speculation and expansion, the Great Crash wiped out billions of dollars of wealth overnight. The Crash began on October 29, 1929, also known as "Black Tuesday." By the time the market bottomed out in 1932, Americans had lost 89 percent of their investments—89 percent!

The Great Crash ushered in the Great Depression. In the mid-20s, real estate prices had reached unheard-of levels. Banks had loaned money to investors, who purchased real estate and stocks. When the banks demanded loans be paid, investors had no money to give. Suddenly, the banks were holding billions of dollars in worthless paper. Depositors demanded their money back. After President Franklin D. Roosevelt declared a "bank holiday" on March 5, 1933, many banks never reopened.

In 1936, Florence Owens Thompson was working as a pea picker in California. At 32 years of age, the worry and desperation in her face made her appear much older than she was and reflected the Great Depression's impact on ordinary Americans.[35]

With the billions in wealth lost in the stock market, in real estate, and in shuttered banks, consumer spending came to a screeching halt. Since consumers were not spending money, businesses were not able to pay employees. Stores and factories closed, and unemployment spiraled out of control. Millions of Americans were unemployed. Men took to the rails to find work—any work—to support their families. Roosevelt created the New Deal to put men back to work, but this was still not enough to counter the effects of speculation and excesses from the early 1920s.

It took a war for the economy to finally recover. The December 7, 1941, attack on Pearl Harbor woke the Sleeping Giant to the conflict raging in Europe and Asia.

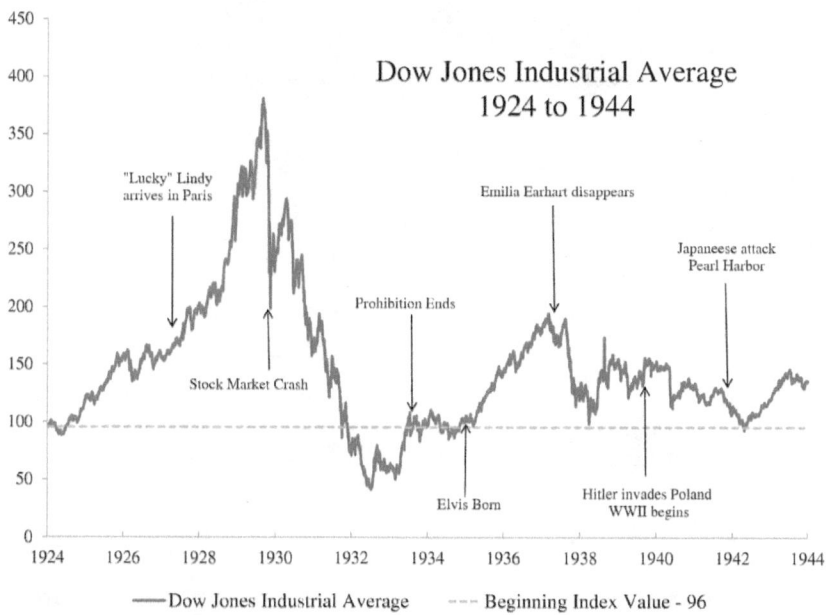

Chart of the Dow Jones Industrial Average from 1924 to 1944. In 1924 the market was at 96; two decades later, it stood at 136.[36]

This Dow Jones Industrial Average chart shows the volatility of those challenging times in American history.

What might surprise many people is that after reaching bottom in 1932, the market experienced one of its largest short-term increases. During the next five years, the Dow grew by 356 percent. How did that happen during the Great Depression? Moreover, after that big increase, why were people still in a depression?

Most investors don't realize how much people have to gain to break even after a big loss. For instance, let's assume that the market drops 20 percent. You might think it would take a 20 percent gain to get your money back. Right? Unfortunately, the math doesn't work that way.

Percentage Lost	Gain to Recover
10%	11%
20%	25%
30%	43%
40%	67%
50%	100%
60%	150%
70%	233%
80%	400%
89%	809%

As you can see in the chart above, a 20 percent loss requires a 25 percent gain for recovery. As losses increase, the necessary gains for getting the money back grow exponentially. To make up the 89 percent loss in the Great Crash, the market would have to grow 809 percent. Twenty-five years would pass before that would happen. As Richard Salsman explains, "Anyone who bought stocks in mid-1929 and held onto them saw most of his or her adult life pass by before getting back to even."[37]

THE GOLDEN AGE OF CAPITALISM: 1944 TO 1964

On V-J Day, a jubilant American sailor clutches a uniformed nurse in a back-bending, passionate kiss, expressing his joy while thousands jam New York City's Times Square to celebrate the long-awaited victory over Japan.[38]

This kiss on V-J Day led to other romantic activities, and the Baby Boom began. After the war, an estimated 77.3 million people were born in the United States.[39]

People had entered the golden age of capitalism, another time of rapid innovation. The world became smaller as commercial air travel became a reality. A new medium—television—would also change the world. In 1946, 0.5 percent of U.S. households had televisions; by 1962, that number had increased to 90 percent.[40]

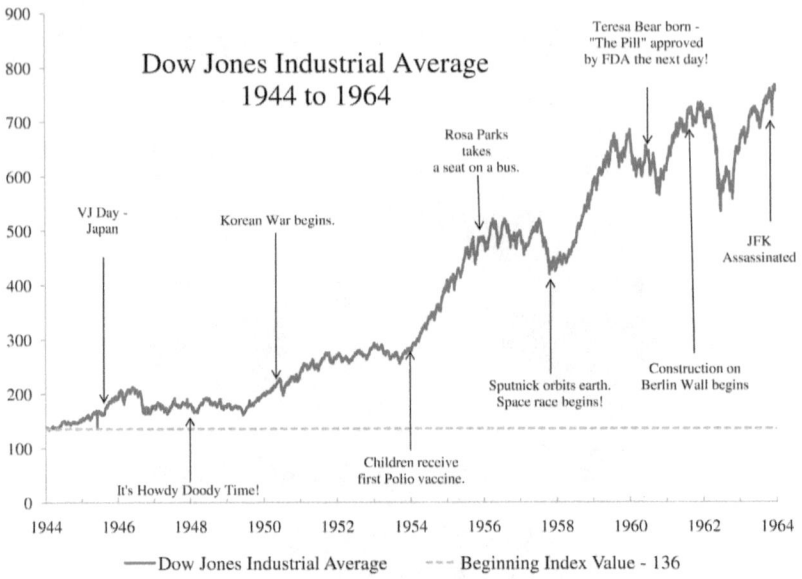

Chart of the Dow Jones Industrial Average from 1944 to 1964. The market began at 136 and ended at 766, growing over 9 percent per year during that time.[41]

The market expanded again: that twenty-year time frame saw an increase of 464 percent.

THE TUMULTUOUS YEARS: 1964 TO 1982

President John F. Kennedy Jr. and First Lady Jacqueline Kennedy, riding in a motorcade with Texas governor John Connally, and his wife, Nellie, shortly before Kennedy's assassination.[42]

Camelot was over: JFK was dead. All Americans knew *exactly* what they were doing on November 22, 1963, when they heard the horrible news that their beloved president had been murdered. Other assassinations, including those of Bobby Kennedy and Martin Luther King Jr., followed. It seemed as if the violence would never end. Thousands of Americans were killed in far-away Vietnam. Blood spilled domestically too as people waged the battle for civil rights in cities throughout the county. For the first time, an American president was impeached and forced to resign in disgrace. America was bruised and brokenhearted.

Likewise, the economy was bruised and brokenhearted. Gas prices soared and double-digit inflation destroyed purchasing power. Double-digit interest rates followed. During the late '70s and early '80s, short-term interest rates ranged between 16 percent and 20 percent. For most young people, the American dream of buying a home raced out of reach; they couldn't afford a mortgage, given the high interest rates.

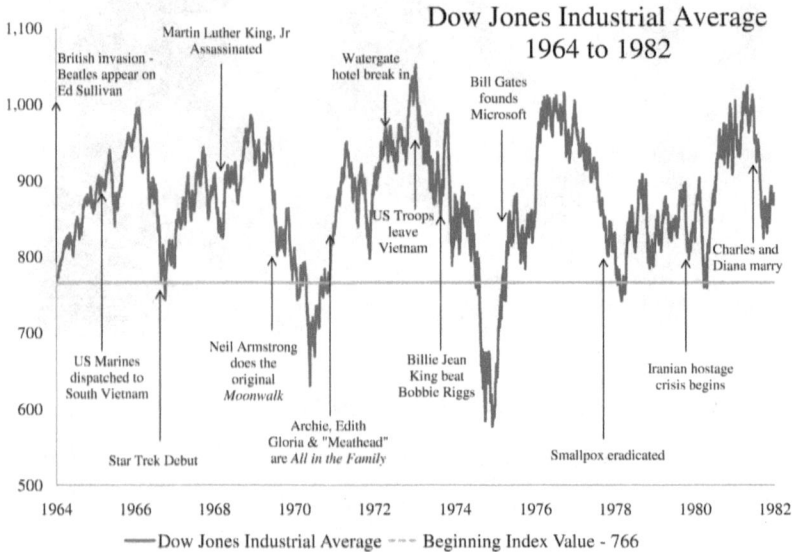

Chart of the Dow Jones Industrial Average from 1964 to 1982. The market started at 766 and ended at 883 eighteen years later. The extended bear market resulted in a mere .79 percent annualized return.[43]

So, what happed to the market? Its changes reflected political and social upheaval. That period saw three recessions. At the beginning of 1982, the market was only slightly higher than it had been eighteen years earlier.

THE INFORMATION AGE: 1982 TO 2000

The space shuttle launch characterized the stock market during the '80s and '90s: they both went straight up.

During the information age—or technology boom—the market zoomed once again. When I started my career as a CPA in the early '80s, my firm had two computers for a staff of twenty-five. To use a computer, you would insert a program disk in floppy drive A and a data disk in floppy drive B.

At that time, a mouse was a little animal you could catch in a spring-loaded trap, not something that resided on your desk. However, during the '80s and '90s, a personal computer moved from a machine that just had floppy drives A and B to a workhorse that boasted more capacity in a single chip than an entire roomful of computers could during the '60s. Soon every office—and many homes—had a computer. Even simple coffee pots had computer chips in them so that they could be programmed to brew your favorite java in the morning.

The information age is when most of you readers made your money, and it's where most of your retirement dollars came from.

Chart of the Dow Jones Industrial Average from 1982 to 2000. This eighteen-year period marked the largest bull market in U.S. history, with an average annual gain of over 15 percent.[44]

During this time, the market made its most impressive gains ever, starting at 882 and ending—when the ball dropped in Times Square at the end of 1999—at 11,497. That's an astounding 1,186 percent increase during the eighteen-year period.

THE NEW MILLENNIUM: 2000 TO PRESENT

Without question, the birth of the Internet was the greatest innovation of the '90s. When PCs began to talk to each other via the World Wide Web, the Internet connected humans the way no other innovation in the history of the world had done. Because of the excitement surrounding this innovation, investors—already giddy over gains in their accounts—began pouring millions of dollars into Internet-related companies. These new companies didn't need to be profitable. They just needed to be connected. Profits were only necessary for "old-fashioned companies." The new economy had new rules.

The dot.com bubble reached its zenith on March 10, 2000, when the technology-heavy NASDAQ index closed at 5,048. During the next two years, however, the tech markets collapsed. In October 2002, the NASDAQ hit bottom. It had fallen 78 percent. Many technology companies went out of business.

When the Times Square clock struck midnight on January 1, 2000, New York City was at the top of the world—epitomized by Lady Liberty, herself, and the Twin Towers' iconic profile on the skyline. Less than two years later, all that changed.

Disaster hit America. Events on September 11, 2001, changed its people forever. Suddenly, we no longer felt safe. Once again, America was at war. After 9/11 and the dot.com crash, the markets have continued to reflect Americans' insecurity.

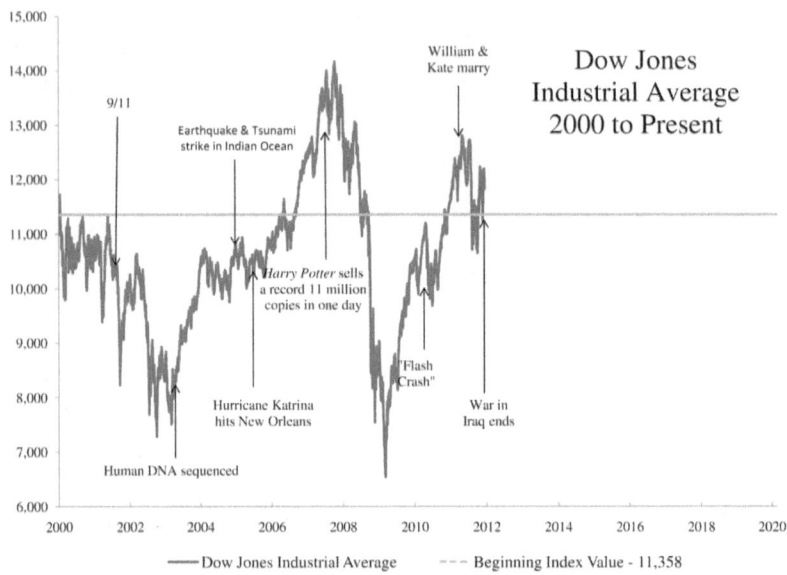

Chart of the Dow Jones Industrial Average from 2000 to 2011. After starting at 10,942, the market has been going sideways for much of the new millennium.[45]

If most investors were to look at where their accounts are today and where those accounts were in 2000, they'd be left wondering, "What happened?" If you followed the advice of most brokers and didn't sell but just held on, you went through about eleven years during which the market went nowhere. Of course, during that time the market didn't stay level; two huge drops occurred. The market went up and down and back up and back down, and now we're still at about the same place as we were eleven years ago.

WHAT SHOULD JILL DO?

If you believe that market history repeats itself, then with our national debt at an all-time high, terrorism still a threat, and our banks still struggling, we may see another eight or ten years during which the market goes nowhere.

So, how do you make money in the midst of all this? The market could be up this year or next year—or it could be another ten years before it goes up again. How do you manage money in the midst of all this when you may not have the time to climb up that stock market hill again? With the state of our economy today, should you be investing in the same way you were a year ago? Should you be investing in the same way you were when working?

CHAPTER 5

THE MANY FLAVORS OF INVESTMENTS

> ### *Once Upon a Time...*
>
> He finally tore his eyes away from the druidess Cliodna, who was scratching her nose, to open a bag of Bertie Bott's Every Flavor Beans.
>
> "You want to be careful with those," Ron warned Harry. "When they say every flavor, they mean every flavor—you know, you get all the ordinary ones, like chocolate and peppermint and marmalade, but then you can get spinach and liver and tripe. George reckons he had a booger-flavored one once."
>
> Ron picked up a green bean, looked at it carefully, and bit into a corner.
>
> "Bleaaargh—see? Sprouts."
>
> They had a good time eating Every Flavor Beans. Harry got toast, coconut, baked bean, strawberry, curry, grass, coffee, sardine, and was even brave enough to nibble the end of a funny gray one Ron wouldn't touch, which turned out to be pepper.

Excerpt from *Harry Potter and the Sorcerer's Stone* by J.K. Rowling[46]

When I was a young girl, I often visited my maternal grandparents, who lived in the thriving metropolis of Mapleton, Kansas. My mother was one of six children. Although neither Mom nor her siblings had that many children, I still had lots of cousins. When we all gathered for the holidays, the rambling farmhouse my grandparents lived in somehow housed more than twenty people.

During those family reunions, my grandfather would sit in his chair and all the grandchildren would eagerly gather at his feet. Many people may have memories of hearing great stories or words of wisdom from their grandfathers. However, Grandpa Needham didn't say much to us. We gathered at his feet out of greed—not love—because he would pitch pennies to us. We cousins always scrambled for the coins with a take-no-prisoners attitude. As a child, I thought that such an early inheritance was a sign of Grandpa's benevolence. As an adult, I think his reasons for bequeathing the riches to his grandchildren were maybe a bit more selfish—to get us out from underfoot.

Immediately after we received our riches from Grandpa, we would swarm out of the house and take the short hike into town. This town had four churches—and only one store. But the store was magical. It had an old-fashioned candy counter and penny candy.

Whenever we entered the store, we were overwhelmed by the multitude of jars behind the counter. There was licorice (both black and red), Pixy Stix, candy cigarettes, saltwater taffy (in an assortment of colors and flavors), candy bracelets, jawbreakers, Bit-O-Honey, wax bottles, Tootsie Rolls, Smarties, Necco Wafers, and peppermint wheels—the choices were endless. The proprietor of the store's patience was equally endless whenever we Needham grandchildren made our selections.

THE MANY FLAVORS OF INVESTMENTS

Most of the time, I was happy with what I got, but occasionally what looked great in the jar did not meet my taste expectations. Fortunately, I never tasted pepper-, liver-, or booger-flavored candy as the witches and wizards in Harry Potter's world did, but I never could understand why anyone would enjoy black licorice.

It can be as hard to choose investments as it was to pick out candy when we were young.

Retirees may feel like kids in a candy story when it comes to investments. There are dizzying arrays of varieties to choose from. Unfortunately, sometimes the investments that look good may end up leaving a bad taste in your mouth.

HIGH-RISK INVESTMENTS

> **Your Fairy Godvisor Says...**
> High-risk investments are those that offer you the most potential for gain, but you have the potential to lose 100 percent of the amount invested.

Venture Capital: I call venture capital the if-only category. When people talk about their investing regrets, they usually say something like this: "If only I had invested in _____ when _____, I would be rich." For instance, someone might say, "If only I had invested in Microsoft when Bill Gates still had pimples, I would be a multimillionaire." The problem is that for all the Microsoft millionaires, or lucky investors, there are many more investors who lost all of their money to a good idea that never caught on.

Personally, I remember my father investing in the Ranger during the mid-60s. The Ranger was an amphibious vehicle designed to function as a car on land and as a boat in water. Ever heard of the Ranger? You probably haven't, because it sunk.

Because of the risk involved in venture capitalism, most investors avoid it. There are almost unlimited upside possibilities, but the unlimited downside potential puts this type of investment in the highest risk category.

Stock: Investment in publically traded, individual stocks is not quite as risky as venture capital, but investors can still lose 100 percent of their money. Who would have thought, even five years ago, that General Motors would be bankrupt today? From 1991 to 2010 the stock market has had an average annual return of 9.14

percent.[47] However, many individual stockowners have not seen that return, or they've lost money on their investments.

MEDIUM RISK

Your Fairy Godvisor Says...
Medium-risk assets are those in which you can lose the principal but are unlikely to lose 100 percent of the dollars you invest.

Mutual Funds and Exchange Traded Funds (ETFs): This category carries less risk than individual stock portfolios do because it holds a diversified basket of stocks and other investments. An investor in this category would not lose 100 percent of her investment unless every company in the fund went bankrupt. However, this diversification benefit comes at a price. Although diversification reduces risk, it also reduces potential return: typically, investors pay fees for the fund's management and trading costs.

Variable Annuities: Variable annuities are invested in subaccounts, which are similar to mutual funds. So, do these accounts have higher or lower fees than mutual funds do? Many people are surprised to find the fees in these accounts are usually much higher than those of mutual funds—sometimes double—and this can really eat into returns.

Bonds: I've met with many investors who are shocked they have lost money in their bond portfolios. They say things like, "I told my broker I wanted out of the stock market. I didn't want to lose money." When you tell your broker that you don't want to take risks, more often than not, her solution is bonds. However, it's really important to understand that when interest rates fall, long-term bond prices rise. In the low-interest rate environment we are currently experiencing, if interest rates increase—unless bonds are held to maturity—bond prices could, potentially, crash to the ground.

NO MARKET RISK

Your Fairy Godvisor Says...
The low-risk category includes accounts that can't lose money due to stock market risk.

Cash and Money Market: Everyone needs to have liquid funds in case of an emergency, so having cash in these accounts is essential for all retirees. However, given the low interest rates in these accounts, you won't be able to even keep up with inflation. That's why, when it comes to their long-term investments, many retirees are turning to other low-risk categories that pay better returns.

CDs: The decline in interest rates from 2008 to 2012 has really hit CD owners hard. Many retirees had or have been relying on income from CDs. Five years ago, you could have found a 5 percent CD, but not anymore. For safe money, most retirees are fleeing from what I call certificates of disappointment in search of better returns.

Fixed Annuities: Fixed annuities are similar to bank CDs in that they pay a fixed rate of interest over a period of time (generally, between five and ten years). Interest rates are typically higher than those of bank CDs or money market accounts, and fixed annuities have the added advantage of being tax-deferred. This means that taxes are not paid on the accounts until the money is withdrawn.

Fixed Indexed Annuities: These are fixed annuities that have their interest rates tied to an index, such as the S&P 500®. Fixed indexed annuities haven't been around as long as other types of investment accounts, so we don't have twenty-year rates of return for them. However, the numbers so far are impressive. In the most comprehensive study performed to date, researchers from the prestigious Wharton School of Business analyzed actual rates of return on fixed indexed annuities from 1997 through 2007. They found that the average five-year annualized rate of return was 5.79 percent.[48] This was earned without taking on any market risk.

Stock market risk is particularly important when you review the performance of each particular investment and how the average investor has done.

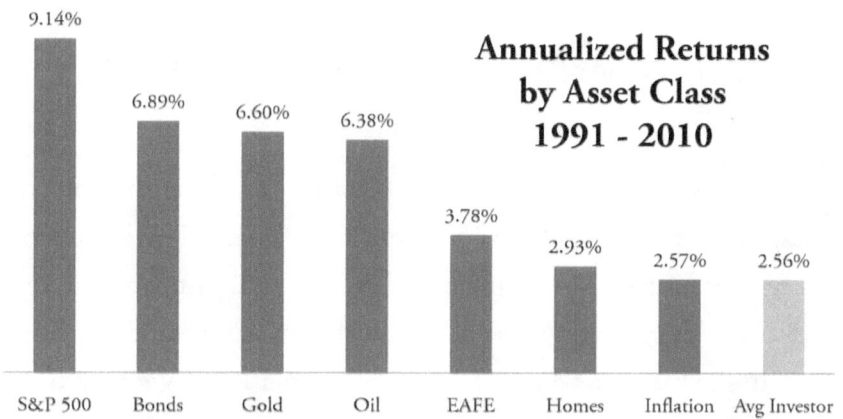

The chart shows how investors' diversified portfolios underperformed in all the major indexes from 1991 to 2010.[49]

The above chart reveals results of a study by the Dalbar Institute, a well-respected market research firm, on the performance of various investments. The study reviewed returns by asset class from January

1991 to December 2010. The performance figures for stocks included nine years of some of the best markets ever (from 1991 to 1999) as well as the stagnant markets from 2000 to 2010. As you can see, the S&P 500® index returned an impressive performance of 9.14 percent.[50]

Grimm Facts

After reviewing the indexes' performance, the Dalbar study further examined how much the average investor earned in her accounts.[51] The results are shocking. The average asset allocation investor in the study only earned a paltry 2.56 percent. This number does not even keep up with the 2.57 percent inflation rate.[52]

THE STOCK MARKET ROLLER COASTER

Why is there such a disparity between actual returns and the average investment portfolio's performance? The key, I believe, is that we are only human. We are tantalized by potential gain. So, when the market is rising, we buy stocks. When the market begins to fall, we listen to the brokers, who say, "It's only a paper loss." We hold on.

As the market continues to fall, the brokers say, "Don't worry. It'll come back; it always does." We hold on.

Finally, when we see our life savings disappearing before our eyes, we demand that our brokers get us out of the stock market. We sell, invariably at or near to the bottom. When the market begins to recover, we wait. It goes up a little more. We wait. Finally, when we are comfortable with the increases, we invest. By that time, we have missed out on most of the recovery.

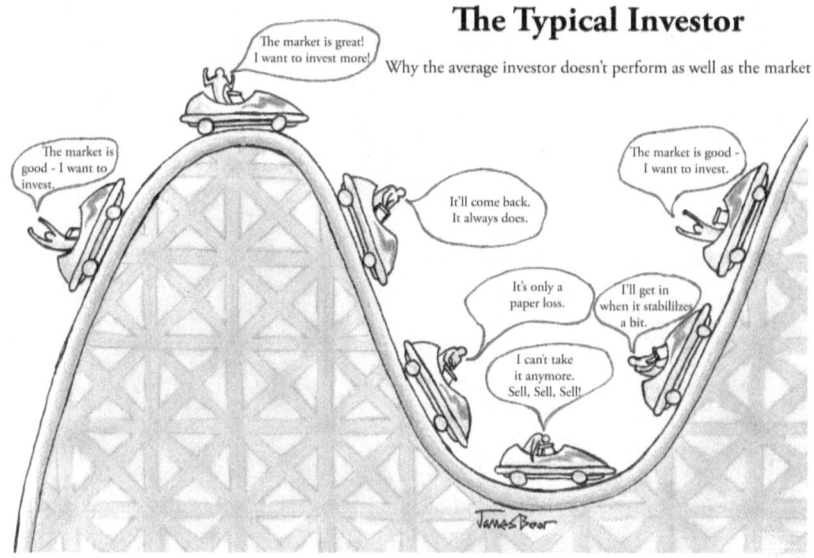

It's almost as if investors are riding a roller coaster—blindfolded. However, on the stock market roller coaster, we never know when we've reached the top or when we've hit bottom.

The last time that I visited a Disney™ theme park, long lines of adolescents and young adults were waiting for a chance to go on the "big" rides: The Twilight Zone™, Tower of Terror™, California Screamin'™, Space Mountain™, and The Matterhorn Bobsleds™. I didn't see many retirees waiting in line, hoping for a chance to be scared on one of those thrill rides. Maybe they outgrew the rides, or maybe they got all the excitement they could stand watching their portfolios go up and down.

THE NAKED TRUTH ABOUT ANNUITIES

"With the golden thread you have furnished us, we have woven the finest garment ever created. Watch how it shimmers and shines. Feel how luxurious it is. This material doesn't weigh you down. It's light and airy, and is guaranteed not to rub or chafe your skin. As tailors to royalty, we understand that royal skin is particularly sensitive.

Notice, as well, the impeccable tailoring. The other royalty we have worked for have all been ecstatic about the perfect fit of our garments. We are positive you'll find this outfit so lightweight, and fitted so perfectly, that wearing it will feel like wearing nothing at all.

When people see you today, they will be amazed. Remember, not everyone can appreciate high-quality fabric. This cloth is not only fit for royalty, but it will also allow you to judge whom you can trust. You see, the cloth is invisible to those who are fools. Trust us, Your Majesty. You look wonderful, and anyone who can't appreciate that is an idiot."

Those were the famous words of the swindlers who cheated an emperor out of the gold used to create a new suit of clothes. Only after a lone voice in the crowd shouted, "He has nothing on," did the emperor realize he had been hoodwinked—and that he was naked.

Sometimes, investors are similarly shocked to discover the accounts they set up to keep themselves covered and warm through retirement are bare. This leaves the investors feeling as though they have been stripped and their fortunes stolen through false promises and deception.

BECKY'S STORY

Becky was very excited about an annuity she had purchased several years previously. Initially, she had invested $500,000 in the account, and the benefit had grown to over $644,000. The salesman had told her the account was guaranteed to never lose money and would grow by 7 percent per year. She thought this was almost too good to be true and felt lucky to have invested in the product. However, when she called the insurance company later to verify the salesmen's claims, she discovered the truth: it was too good to be true.

Becky found out she was only promised a return of the initial investment when she died. The 7 percent growth was not on money she could withdraw or spend as she liked, but only a calculator for a potential future income. In fact, the real account balance had dropped by over $90,000. The only way for Becky to get all of the money back while she was alive was for the stock market to increase enough to offset those losses, or for her to live long enough to recover her losses through the benefit.

The biggest surprise for Becky was finding that as long as she owned the account, she was paying the insurance company almost $13,000 in fees each and every year—paying them to lose her money. Becky was shocked to find out that, like the emperor, she was naked.

Your Fairy Godvisor Says...

Sadly, Becky was also not told about the strings attached to her account. It is vitally important that you know about the strings attached to any annuity (or any other investment). All annuities have strings attached. You have the right to know what the strings are in order to evaluate whether the account is right for you.

THE NAKED TRUTH ABOUT ANNUITIES

First of all, there is nothing inherently good or bad about annuities in general. Insurance companies issue all annuities. That is generally a good thing, since insurance companies are heavily regulated and conservatively managed. If the name of the company that holds your account includes the word insurance, then you probably own an annuity.

Another great thing about annuities is that they can be designed to provide income for life. This is very important to at least 61 percent of the population,[53] who fear running out of money more than they fear death.

> our Fairy Godvisor Says...
>
> The FDIC does not insure annuities. All annuity guarantees are backed by the claims-paying ability of the issuing insurance company.

We can break annuities into two broad category types: immediate and deferred.

The Naked Truth About Annuities!

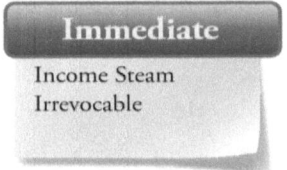

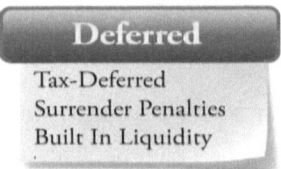

IMMEDIATE ANNUITIES

Immediate annuities have the benefit of providing investors with lifetime income. They work much like pensions and are often called pension-type annuities.

Suppose Peggy has just turned sixty-five and wants to receive income for the rest of her life. Upon investigation, she finds she can invest $100,000 in an immediate annuity and receive a monthly check of $538 for the rest of her life.[54] The good news about this type of annuity is that if she lives to be eighty-one years old, she will get her principal back. If she lives to be one hundred, she will receive payments of $226,163—not a bad return on the $100,000 initial investment.

Now, for the bad news. An immediate annuity is irrevocable. After the payments begin, if Peggy passes away, the insurance company keeps the money and the benefits cease. For this reason, Peggy decides she's not comfortable with this type of annuity. She wants an annuity that will allow for her money to be passed on to her children if she doesn't live long enough to collect all the benefits. She decides to look for another type of annuity, which turns out to be more popular: a deferred annuity.

DEFERRED ANNUITY

One great thing about owning a deferred annuity is that this type of annuity is tax-deferred. That means an investor doesn't have to pay tax on the annuity earnings until she takes money out of the account. (Of course, tax-qualified annuities, such as tax-sheltered annuities and IRA annuities, are already tax-deferred). Most individuals feel it's important to keep money out of the hands of Uncle Sam for as long as possible. A good deferred annuity will allow an account to grow and defer tax until the investor needs income sometime in the future.

One of the strings attached to a deferred annuity is time. These are not short-term investments; they are designed for long-term planning. If you withdraw money from one of these accounts before the end of the surrender period, the insurance company imposes a penalty.

Although annuities are long-term investments (generally with terms of five years or more), most allow for withdrawals prior to the end of the surrender period. After the first year, almost all annuities allow investors to remove up to 10 percent of the account balance each year without incurring a penalty. Certain accounts allow for additional withdrawals in case of confinement, terminal illness, or death of the contract holder.

The spectrum of deferred annuities has two subcategories: variable and fixed.

The Naked Truth About Annuities!

Immediate
Income Stream
Irrevocable

Deferred
Tax-Deferred
Surrender Penalties
Built In Liquidity

Fixed
Principal Guaranteed

Variable
Invest in Market
Can Lose Money
Fees Involved

WHAT IS A VARIABLE ANNUITY?

A variable annuity is the type of annuity in which Becky invested, as described in the story above. What does financial author Suze Orman think of this type of annuity? Ms. Orman was asked, "My financial advisor is recommending that I buy a variable annuity within my retirement account. What should I do?"

Her reply was, "Get yourself another financial advisor, pronto."[55]

I agree with Orman. If we analyze Becky's account in more depth, we discover several scary things.

SAFETY

Most variable annuities are not safe. You can lose the principal, since a variable annuity is a direct investment in the stock market. It is invested in subaccounts, which are similar to mutual funds. So, when the market goes up, your account goes up. When the market goes down, your account goes down.

HIGH FEES

In a variable annuity, the only guarantee that you will receive your initial investment back is if you die. Most insurance companies charge a fee, called a mortality-and-expense (M&E) fee, for that guarantee. In Becky's case, the M&E fee was 1.4 percent.

Imagine walking into a bank and informing your teller you want a safe investment. The friendly banker, Henry, tells you that you must leave your money in the account for seven years before you can withdraw the balance. He says the bank will deduct a fee of 1.4 percent each year. In return for that fee, the bank promises that if you die, your beneficiaries will get all the money you invested. You look at Henry, amazed, and say, "You mean that I pay you 1.4 percent annually, and the only guarantee is that 100 percent of my money is returned when I die? What kind of a deal is that? I think I'll take my money elsewhere."

Additionally, many insurance companies charge an annual administrative fee of up to .25 percent. What, exactly, does the administration fee cover? As far as I can tell, the administrative fee covers printing of your monthly statements. So, for an account worth $100,000, the annual fee is $250. This seems excessive for a few sheets of paper and a stamp.

> ## Your Fairy Godvisor Says...
>
> Other types of fees—that are, generally, only disclosed in the contract's fine print—include mutual fund management fees. Since variable annuities are invested in subaccounts, the managers of the funds demand compensation for their investment expertise. These subaccount fees can vary widely but generally are about .8 percent to 1 percent of the account balance.[56]

Finally, most variable annuity contracts offer riders that add benefits to the contract. In most cases, these are benefits that you pay for, which add to the policy's cost. If you hear the term rider in relation to any insurance account, think fees.

For her variable annuity, Becky's account fees were as follows:

M&E Fee	1.40%
Subaccount Expense	1.00%
Income Rider	0.75%
Total Fees	3.15%

Based on her account's value at the time, Becky was paying a whopping 3.15 percent in fees for this account each and every year: $12,902 for one year alone. That translates into $129,020 over a ten-year period.

GUARANTEED LIFETIME WITHDRAWAL BENEFITS: INCOME BENEFITS

Income riders work wonders for retirees who are worried about outliving their money and need a monthly income check. Those payments are based on the income benefit's base, sometimes called the GLWB (Guaranteed Lifetime Withdrawal Benefit).

In Becky's case, the benefit base grew at a rate of 7 percent per year. When Becky began receiving her income payments, the benefit base would be used to calculate the monthly income check's amount. However, the income base's amount (the GLWB) is not real money that can be withdrawn, as a lump sum, from the account.

I remember playing *Monopoly*™ as a child. We used *Monopoly*™ money for the game. Everyone knew that *Monopoly*™ money was not real money. It only worked inside the game.

To understand how Becky's account worked, we need to analyze three important numbers:

Initial Investment/Death Benefit	$500,000
Accumulation Value/"Real Money"	$409,589
GLWB/"Monopoly™ Money"	$644,622

Initial Investment ($500,000): This was the initial contribution Becky made to the account. It is also the minimum the insurance company would pay in the event of Becky's death, assuming no withdrawals are taken.

Accumulation Value ($409,580): The accumulation value is the investment's real money value, the amount Becky could walk away with at the end of the term. This amount includes earnings, minus any fees and withdrawals. It can be higher or lower than the initial investment. If the stock market had been good to Becky, she would have been able to withdraw a higher balance. Unfortunately for Becky, stock market losses and fees ate into her accumulation value, and she lost money on her investment.

GLWB (Guaranteed Lifetime Withdrawal Benefit) or "*Monopoly*™ Money"($644,622): This number is what I call "*Monopoly*™ money." This money cannot be withdrawn as a lump sum at any time. It is only used to calculate future income payments. This calculation is not standard; it varies by company and by contract.

Income accounts are not necessarily bad; they can be very helpful for generating income in retirement. The sad thing in Becky's case is that the difference between real money and *Monopoly*™ money was not explained to her when the salesman sold her the original account. Becky was shocked because she thought the account was worth $644,622, while the actual value was only $409,589. She was devastated to discover her account was worth $235,000 less than she thought it was.

A SAFER OPTION: THE FIXED ANNUITY

A safer alternative to a variable annuity is a fixed annuity. In a fixed annuity, the principal is insured against market losses.

There are two types of fixed annuities: traditional and indexed. They suit different types of investors.

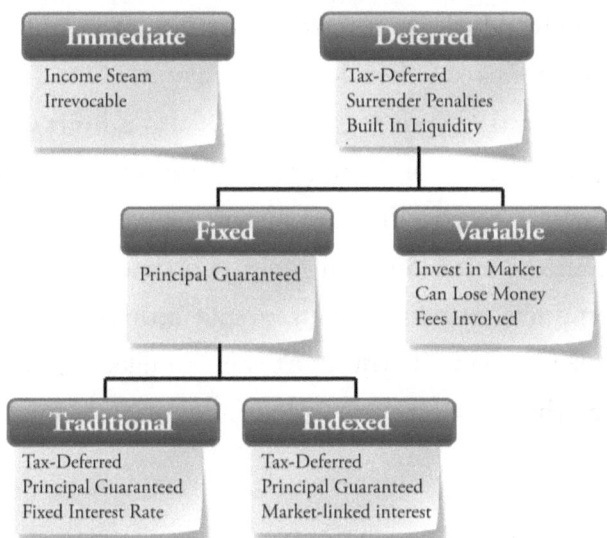

Traditional Fixed Annuities: Joan was a CD buyer. She liked the fixed interest rate and the insurance protection, but hated paying taxes every year on money she was simply reinvesting. So, a traditional fixed annuity fits her perfectly. Her investment earns a fixed interest rate that is higher than what her local bank was paying; it's insured; and best of all, she doesn't have to pay tax on the interest every year.

Fixed Indexed Annuities (or Hybrid Annuities): Sandra wanted a higher return than what the fixed annuity paid. She liked the higher potential returns from investing in the stock market but didn't want to lose her principal. In a fixed indexed annuity, the interest earned is tied to the performance of a market index, such as the S&P 500®. If the index goes up, Sandra's account goes up. If the index falls, Sandra doesn't earn anything during the year, but she doesn't lose any of her principal, either.

These annuities were developed for the investors who wanted safety while also having the potential to earn a higher return than they might with other safe investment options. You still need to be aware of the strings attached to these accounts. One string is that in return for limiting your losses, there is also a limit on the gains you can earn. You must also agree to hold the annuity for a set time period in order to receive the most benefit.

A qualified professional can help you determine where these types of products best fit in your overall retirement plan. In the words of Suze Orman, "If you don't want to take any risks but still want to play the stock market, a good index annuity might be right for you."[57]

FINDING A DESIRABLE ANNUITY

When searching for the best annuity, you can use the following chart, which shows how to tell a desirable annuity from an undesirable one.

Desirable	Undesirable
10-Year Term or Less	16-, 18-, or 20-Year Term
Fees for Something	Fees for Nothing
Good Economics	Poor Economics

ANNUITY TERMS

Most annuities have terms between five and ten years (known as the surrender period). However, I have seen terms on annuities ranging from sixteen to twenty years. In my opinion, this is way too long. If you can't hold the annuity for the entire term (unless you are using it for estate-planning purposes), it's best to search for other investment options.

FEES FOR SOMETHING

What about fees? Should you pay a fee? Well, the answer is: it depends.

Here's what I mean. Say Lucy's car was falling apart and she decided she wanted to get a new, more reliable vehicle. At the car lot, Frank, the salesman, quoted her a base sticker price of $20,000 for the new car. He said there were several extra charges: $2,000 for the engine, $1,000 for the transmission, and $1,000 for a "luxury combo," which included leather seats, a sunroof, and the latest sound system. Lucy was really annoyed that Frank was adding additional charges for the engine and the transmission. After all, those should be standard equipment included in the base sticker price.

With a variable annuity, you pay extra fees for the "base model," such as mortality and expense fees and administrative fees. *None* of these fees are included in a traditional fixed annuity. However, Lucy might want to add the equivalent of a luxury combo, such as the valuable provision of additional lifetime income benefits, to a fixed annuity. The good news is that in a fixed annuity, such expenses are optional. In fixed annuities, you pay "fees for something" versus "fees for nothing." You only pay for what you want and need.

GOOD ECONOMICS VERSUS BAD ECONOMICS

Investors should always get the best deals for their hard-earned dollars. With that in mind, let's divide investors into two categories: those who are risk-takers and those concerned with protecting the principal.

Risk Takers: Investors who want to make the maximum return and aren't afraid to lose their principal are often sold variable annuities. However, if we look more closely, we find that these economics don't make much sense. While variable annuities provide the greatest upside potential—that is, in good market conditions—the fees weigh down investment returns. If you want the best deal that corresponds to the amount of risk you're taking, buy stocks or stock mutual funds.

So, when is a variable annuity a good investment? According to Suze Orman, "[A variable annuity] *may* be an advantageous investment only if you like to trade—that is, buy and sell—mutual funds often, won't need your money for years to come, and are in a very high tax bracket now but plan to be in a much lower tax bracket at retirement."[58]

Since only a miniscule number of investors purchasing variable annuities meet the above criteria, investing in a variable annuity is often just bad economics.

Safety-Conscious Investors: For these investors, a fixed annuity generally works the best. Such annuities provide safety of principal and a greater upside potential than other fixed income accounts do. They have good economics when compared to other safe investments or other annuities.

CHAPTER 7
THE QUEST FOR THE PERFECT INVESTMENT

Once Upon a Time...
"Your wish is my command," said the genie to his new mistress.

"Wow, did you come through!" the woman replied. "I wanted a safe investment with a great rate of return that I wasn't locked into long-term. I'm amazed with what you got me. Here's a three-month CD from the Arizona Bank paying an amazing 14 percent interest rate. You are a magical genie. My banker sure couldn't come up with this deal. Thank you so much."

"You are welcome, mistress."

"But ... something is a little off here. I haven't heard of the Arizona Bank in years. Didn't Bank of America buy them out in the '80s?[59] Wait! The date on this CD is April 1, 1982. What's going on?"

"Why, mistress, we've returned to 1982, when you could get a three-month CD paying 14 percent interest. I only did what you asked me to do."

"1982? I can't go back and invest in 1982. I didn't have any money to invest. I was saving for the kids' college. The girls were still teenagers. Teenagers! Oh, my heavens. I can't go through that again. Please, genie, I wish to go back to the future."

"Your wish is my command."

Poof!

"Okay, Genie. Just give me a safe place to invest my money—today. I don't want to lose it."

"Your wish is my command."

Poof!

THREE INVESTING WISHES

Investors have three wishes when it comes to their money.
1. High return
2. High liquidity
3. Low risk

The first wish is a high return on their investments. Of course, investors want to get the best possible rate of return. However, finding high returns is illusive and potentially dangerous. High returns often come at a price: high risk.

Liquidity, which is how easily an asset can be converted to cash, is another issue for investors. For example, currently in Arizona real estate is one of the most non-liquid assets around. Most neighborhoods have several homes foreclosed on by the banks, and these homes are being sold at fire-sale prices. Real estate is a buyer's market and most sellers take large losses if they need to generate cash.

For many retirees, safety is a final concern. When they invest, they don't want to lose the principal, particularly if they are depending upon the income for living expenses.

Unfortunately, short of finding a genie in a bottle, investors can't have all three wishes come true. You can pick one category to focus on—possibly two—and life will dictate the third. Since, at this time, there's no way of getting a 14 percent rate of return on a short-term investment while encountering no risk—except by returning to 1982—it's important to focus on balancing liquidity and rate of return while keeping your assets safe.

THREE WAYS OF SAFELY INVESTING

There are three types of investments people have used in the past to generate "safe" returns: the Wall Street Way, the Bank Way, and the Insurance Way. Let's examine each of them.

THE WALL STREET WAY

To protect their clients—investors who want to avoid the risk of stocks—big brokerage firms turn to bonds.

Bonds come in many "flavors." They can be short-term or long-term and are issued by both corporations and governments. The U.S. government, local governments, and foreign governments can all issue government bonds. Bonds are loans. If you buy a bond, you are lending money to the bond's issuer. The issuer agrees to pay you interest (the "coupon rate") and the principal at a future date ("the maturity date").

Bonds are often referred to as fixed-income investments. This is because—usually—the interest rate is fixed: in other words, the interest rate doesn't change over the life of the loan. While the income doesn't change, though, the principal value of the bond can vary widely. Here's the problem: by seeing bonds as fixed-income investments, investors are often lulled into the false sense of security that the bond is safe and they can't lose the principal. Unfortunately, this perception is not reality. Bonds are subject to two big risks: default risk and interest rate risk.

DEFAULT RISK

Default risk is the risk that the debt may not be repaid. In recent news, much has been made of the debt issues of foreign governments—particularly those of Portugal, Ireland, Greece, and Spain. Closer to home, our own United States Treasuries have lost their AAA rating, according to the Standard and Poor rating agency; they are now only AA+, which is still a great rating, and the United States is not in immediate danger of default. However, we have seen several other defaults over the past few years. Ten years ago, who would have thought that General Motors, one of the largest companies in the United States, would be bankrupt today? Bonds are considered safer than stocks because if a company goes bankrupt, bondholders are paid before the stockholders are. However, in GM's case, bondholders will end up receiving pennies on the dollar, not the nice safe investment that they had planned on.

INTEREST RATE RISK

The second—and larger—risk for bondholders is interest rate risk. Bonds are sensitive to fluctuations in interest rates. To illustrate how bond prices work, let's imagine a seesaw with bond prices on one side and interest rates on the other.

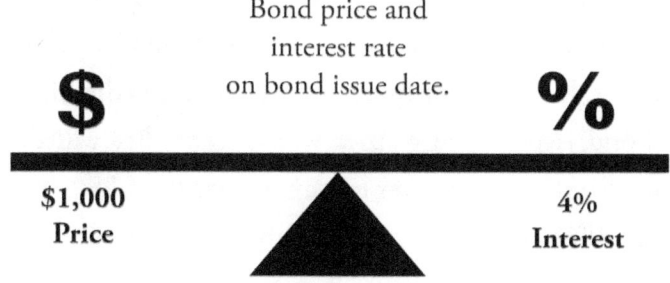

When we were children, we would play on seesaws with our friends. When we clambered aboard, the seesaw became parallel to the ground. Similarly, when a bond is issued, its "seesaw" is flat. In this example, the interest rate is 4 percent and the price per bond is $1,000. When the bond comes due, the company will pay $1,000 to the bondholder. On the issue date and the redemption date, the bonds are balanced and at equilibrium.

However, between these two dates, the seesaw goes up and down according to fluctuating interest rates.

FALLING INTEREST RATES

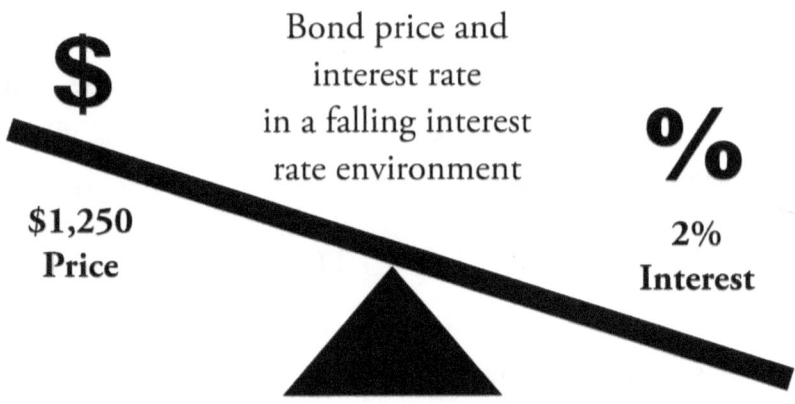

So, what happens in a falling interest rate environment? Let's assume interest rates are now 2 percent. Well, that bond is still paying 4 percent interest. So, if the bond's owner wants to sell it on the open market, she will want to be compensated for the high interest rate the bond is paying. In other words, the seller will demand a "premium" for the bond. Then it may be worth $1,250, as opposed to the original $1,000. We have seen similar increases in bond prices during the past few years because interest rates have been falling.

RISING INTEREST RATES

Will interest rates continue to decrease? I don't have a crystal ball, but, since we are at historic lows for interest rates, I would guess that at sometime in the future, interest rates will rise again. What happens to bond prices then? Let's return to the seesaw example. I remember playing on a seesaw with a not-so-nice friend when I was young. I was at the top and she was at the bottom. She decided to play a trick on me and bail out. All of a sudden, I came crashing to the ground. Ouch! My "friend" had become a literal pain in the rear end.

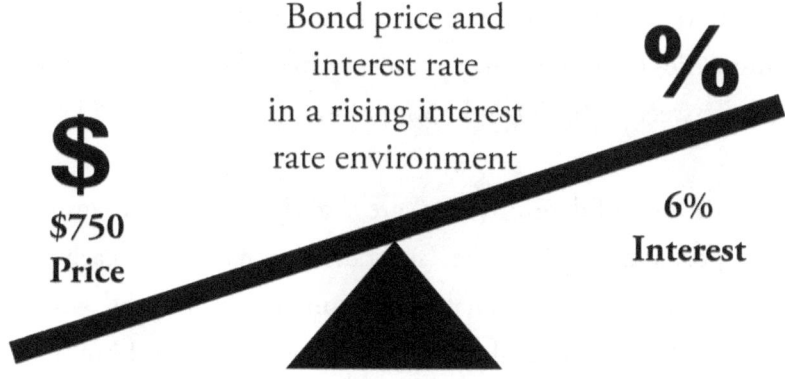

If interest rates go up, long-term bond prices will come crashing to the ground, just like on the seesaw. As a result, unless bonds are held to maturity, the Wall Street Way of investing "safely" may not be so safe in today's low-interest rate environment.

THE BANK WAY

The second way to invest safely is the Bank Way. The U.S. banking system is unique. Unlike what happens at foreign banks, the Federal Deposit Insurance Corporation (FDIC) insures U.S. bank deposits.

That means bank accounts are backed by the full faith and credit of the U.S. government. When a bank goes under, the FDIC reimburses that bank's depositors. Subject to insurance limitations (currently $250,000 per person), no one has lost money when an FDIC-insured bank went bankrupt.

Bank deposits are also highly liquid investments. All investors should have an emergency fund or funds they can access. The amount varies by individual, but most retirees should consider maintaining between $10,000 and $50,000 in bank checking and savings accounts.

Certificates of deposit (CDs) are slightly less liquid than regular bank deposits, since there are "substantial penalties for early withdrawal." Typically, these penalties amount to six months' worth of interest. CDs are a good alternative for emergency fund holdings as they pay a slightly higher interest rate than savings accounts do.

Grimm Facts

Bank CD rates have plummeted over the past few years.

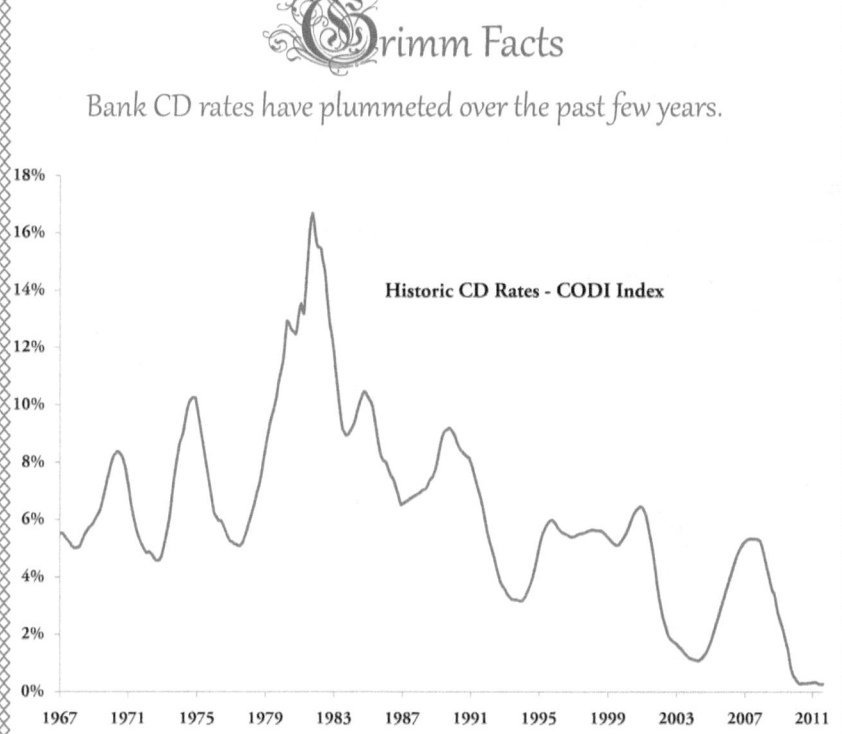

Three-month CD rates from January 1967 to present. Rates peaked at 16.691 in October 1981 and reached a low of .2633 percent in August 2011. The average rate over that period was 6.17 percent.[60]

The 2008 crash devastated CD investors. Retirees who depended upon their CDs paying 5 to 6 percent have seen their incomes slashed. It's difficult to know where to turn. What can an investor do?

THE INSURANCE WAY: FIXED ANNUITIES

Insurance companies also provide safe havens for investors: fixed annuities. A fixed annuity is not the same as a variable annuity, which we discussed in Chapter 6. Fixed annuities come with insurance company guarantees that investors will not lose the principal—if, that is, the investors play by the rules. There are strings attached to these accounts; there are rules to the game that must be followed.

The major string attached to a fixed annuity is time. When you purchase a fixed annuity, you promise to invest with the insurance company for a period of time. If you pull your money out too soon, you will pay what's called a surrender penalty.

Your Fairy Godvisor Says...

You should never invest all your money in a fixed annuity (or in any other single investment, for that matter). You should always have money set aside, in a very liquid bank or money market account for emergencies.

HOW SAFE ARE FIXED ANNUITIES?

Most people would say FDIC-insured bank accounts are just about the safest investments around. The FDIC is an insurance company. In exchange for the insurance protection it offers, individual banks pay premiums to the FDIC. Currently, the FDIC has reserves of less than two cents for every dollar of deposits.

FDIC Insurance Protection

 =

Dollar of Deposit   **FDIC Reserves**

The FDIC is required to maintain 1.35 cents of reserves to cover each dollar on deposit at member banks.[61]

Annuity Insurance Protection

 =

Account Withdrawal Value   **Insurance Company Reserves**

Federal law requires insurance companies to have $1 in reserves to cover each $1 of account withdrawal value: "state law also requires surplus capital be available to increase your protection, as well as contributions to state guaranty funds that provide additional security in the event of unforeseeable problems."[62]

Insurance companies have greater reserves than the FDIC, which are important to protect their fixed annuity investors.

The other advantage insurance products have over bank CDs is the tax advantage. Annuities grow in a tax-deferred manner, so investors don't pay taxes until they withdraw funds from the annuities. This tax savings can make a huge difference to your "safe" money investments.

	Corporate Bonds	Bank Accounts	Fixed Annuities
Fixed interest rate	✓	✓	✓
Highly liquid	✓	✓	
Insurance for each $1 of withdrawal value	No Insurance	🪙	💵
Principal protected from fluctuating interest rates		✓	✓
Principal protected from issuer default		✓	✓
Tax deferred growth			✓

In summary, fixed annuities are the clear winners for long-term investors in terms of safety and tax-deferred growth.

WHAT ABOUT A HIGHER RETURN?

For investors seeking a higher return than what is offered through a fixed annuity, insurance companies have developed "hybrid annuities." Hybrid annuities offer all the benefits shown above, along with potentially higher rates of return. They are also called fixed indexed annuities because they pay higher interest rates based on the performance of some financial indexes. Similar to a regular fixed annuity, one of the strings attached to a fixed indexed annuity is time (usually a period between five and ten years).

The second string attached to a fixed indexed annuity is a limit to the amount of interest you can earn. If you think about it, this limit makes sense.

Your Fairy Godvisor Says...

There's no investment in the world that can guarantee unlimited gains with no potential for losses. (If someone tries to sell you some such account, run as fast as you can—and report him or her to the authorities). Protection always comes at a price.

HOW DO THESE HYBRID ANNUITIES WORK?

Let's assume that CD rates have returned to more "normal" levels and are paying 5 percent. In the example below, the fixed annuity gains are based on Standard and Poor's stock market index (the S&P 500®). For this illustration, let's assume that the most you could make on this account is 10 percent each year. Let's also assume that on the day you opened the account, the S&P 500® index was at 1,000 and you invested $100,000.

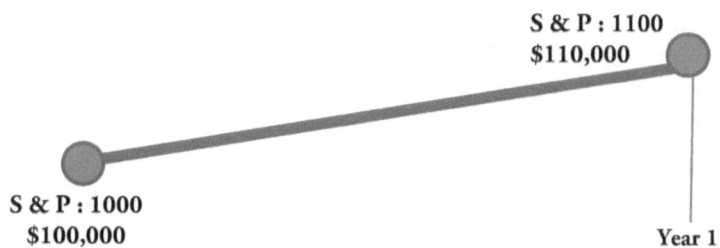

During the first year you owned the account, the market went up 10 percent to 1,100. Your investment went up 10 percent as well to $110,000.[63]

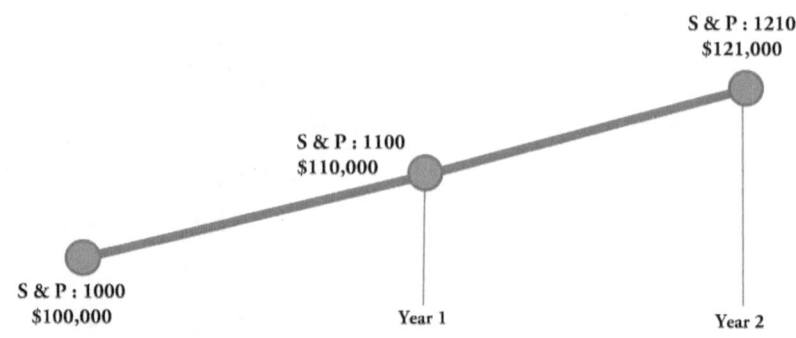

The second year was also a great year for stocks. The market went up another 10 percent, so your investment also grew 10 percent—reaching $121,000.[64]

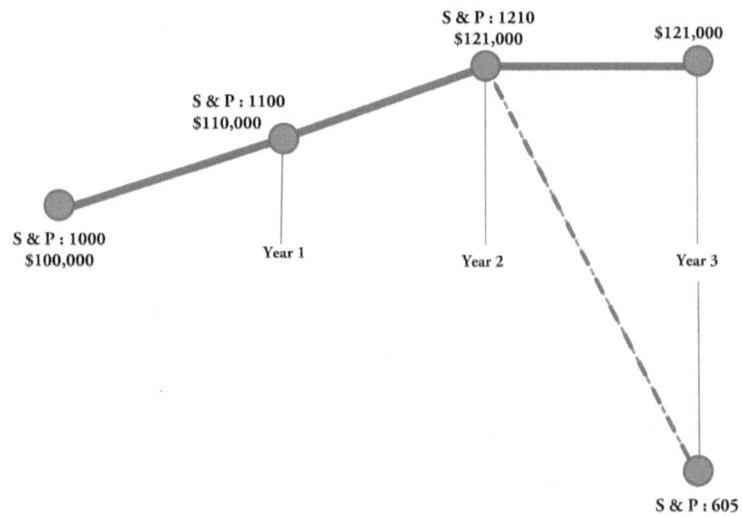

Does the stock market always go up? No. During the third year the market crashed and dropped in half. The S&P 500® index reached 605. So, what happened to your account's value? Well, I have good news and bad news. The bad news is you didn't make one dime with your account during the third year. Zip. Nothing. Nada. You still have the same $121,000 you had in your account at the end of year two.[65]

However, the good news is you didn't lose any money, either. Your investment value locks in each year. The worst-case scenario is that when the market falls, your investment will not make any money. So, the good news is the same as the bad news. You still have the same $121,000 you had in your account at the end of year two.

You might be bummed out about not making any money with this account during the down years. There is, however, a wonderful consolation prize when the stock market crashes. We all want to buy low and sell high, right? Well, no one can perfectly time the markets and always buy at the bottom and sell at the top. Yet these accounts allow you to start over every year at wherever the market's current rate is. So, if the market is low, you get to buy low.

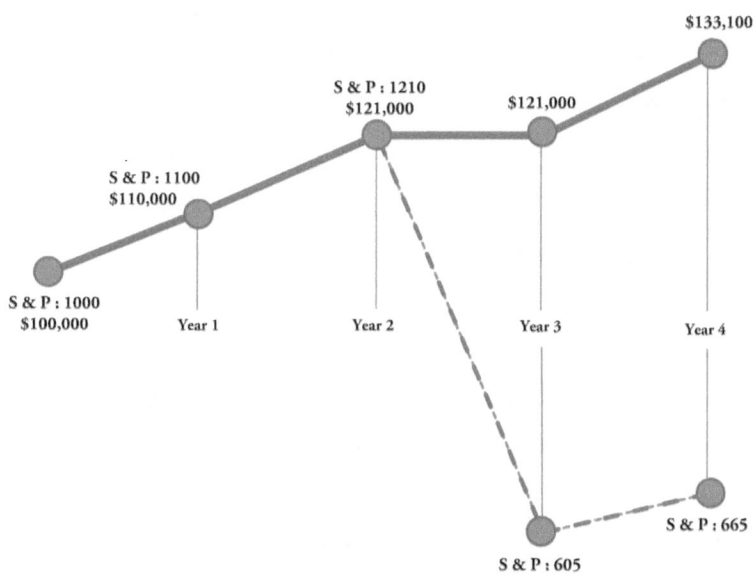

At the beginning of year four, the market index is at a miserable 605. However, since the stock market index locks in each year on your purchase anniversary, your new starting point is that low figure of 605. Let's assume the market partially recovered from the crash in year four and increased another 10 percent, going up to 665. The market is way below where it was when you started, and is still significantly below where it was at the top, but your investment is still higher. You now have $133,100. If you had invested in an S&P 500® index fund, you would only have $66,500.[66]

WHAT ABOUT LIQUIDITY?: "CAN I GET TO MY MONEY IN AN EMERGENCY?"

As I mentioned earlier, you should always have a liquid emergency fund. Some investors are concerned about "tying up" their money for five or ten years in an annuity. "What if there's a big emergency?" they ask. "Isn't an annuity not liquid?"

Let's assume that you had made two investments—one in an S&P 500® index fund and one in the above-mentioned fixed annuity. The S&P 500® index fund can be bought or sold for a nominal fee and is highly liquid. By contrast, many fixed annuities have surrender penalties of 10 to 12 percent during the investment's early years. Typically, surrender fees decrease over the account's holding period. At face value, the S&P 500® index fund is the more liquid investment.

However, what if you had an emergency at the end of year three and needed to withdraw your investment? Your index fund would be worth $60,500, and you would have no surrender charges. Assuming the surrender charge for the annuity is 10 percent, you would lose $12,100 by cashing in the account early, reducing it from $121,000 to $108,900. Which would you prefer having: the $60,500 from your liquid stocks or the $108,900 from the annuity?

INTEREST RATES: A FINAL WORD

Please note that these types of accounts are extremely sensitive to interest rates. Currently, there are no index annuities that pay a 10 percent rate of return—I used this figure for ease of illustration. By using these accounts, on average, you can expect to earn somewhere between what CDs are paying and how the market is performing (without the losses). Many retirees would probably agree with Mark Twain's purported statement: "I am more concerned about the return *of* my money than the return *on* my money."

Building a Brick (Income) House

> ## Once Upon a Time...
>
> Three sisters wanted to build themselves comfortable retirement homes. They wanted to ensure they would be warm, cozy, and protected.
>
> The first sister, Sally Stock, decided to build her house out of straw. The second, Betty Bonds, decided to build her house out of sticks. The third, Irene Income, decided to build her house out of bricks.
>
> Well, pretty soon, the big bad wolf came to visit them. He threatened to huff and puff and blow their houses in. The wolf succeeded with Sally and Betty—they had to move in with their children. Only Irene was able to remain independent and live in her nice, safe home.
>
>

When we retire, we enter a new phase in life. Once we have stopped receiving paychecks, we need to create paychecks from our assets. Unfortunately, the strategies used to accumulate a nest egg do not always work as well when we are spending that nest egg.

SALLY'S HOUSE

According to the standard formula used by most financial planners, if you don't draw more than 4 percent from your retirement accounts per year, you have an 89 percent chance your money will last thirty years.[67] This formula is generally referred to as the Monte Carlo Analysis. (It seems scary to me that brokers use the most famous casino in the world to predict if their clients will have enough income in retirement.)

Assuming Sally followed this formula, she should have had a comfortable retirement. So, what happened? Why did she end up homeless?

The Monte Carlo Analysis assumes "normal" stock market performance. Have the last ten years been "normal"? I don't think so. An interesting study done by T. Rowe Price put the Monte Carlo Analysis to a test, seeing what the likely outcomes would be based on actual stock market results since 2000.

Let's assume that Sally started with $500,000 (with a conservative mix of 55 percent stocks and 45 percent bonds). Beginning at the turn of the century, she withdrew 4 percent of her account balance every year (that is, $1,667 each month). She also took annual "raises" of 3 percent to keep up with inflation. Unfortunately, since the stock market has been anything but normal over the last ten years, according to the study, Sally now has only a 29 percent probability that she will have enough money to last the full thirty years.[68] What a huge drop! No wonder she's forced to move in with her kids.

BETTY'S HOUSE

Betty was a little more cautious than her sister and decided that bonds were a safer alternative, particularly after that first big market loss in October 2002. She had initially invested her money as Sally had, but got scared after the crash. So, she called her broker and said, "Get me out of the stock market. I want safety." Her broker promptly sold all of her stocks and invested the money in bonds.

So, according to the T. Rowe Price study, how has Betty fared? She definitely avoided the crash of 2008, so she should be better off, right? Wrong! According to the study, Betty is doomed—she has a 100 percent chance of running out of money.[69] This is because of her need to continually draw income from accounts that have substantially declined in value.

The most amazing thing about the study is that it was actually published in the company's quarterly report, since T. Rowe Price sells both stock and bond mutual funds.

IRENE'S HOUSE

Irene also wanted a safe, sturdy house. Using the sophisticated income planning tools and investment vehicles available to her, she was able to start out at a higher income level, receiving $1,851 per month instead of $1,667 per month.[70] Irene has really appreciated that extra $184 each month. Additionally, she has been assured this income will last her entire life—even if she lives to be as old as Besse

Cooper, who, at 114, is currently the oldest woman living in the United States.

> **Warning:** *This book frequently uses very specific annuities to generate the income illustrated above. You, the reader, should not view the comments here as a blanket endorsement of all annuity contracts.*

In a groundbreaking publication, W. Van Harlow, Ph.D., suggests the greatest threat to a retiree's portfolio is an unfavorable "sequence-of-returns risk," adding, "[i]f a retiree is unfortunate enough to be exposed to a sequence of adverse returns early in retirement, the likelihood of an early depletion of savings rises dramatically."[71]

What this means is if there is a bear market in the early years of your retirement, then your funds will be depleted and you risk running out of money. This is the same conclusion drawn in the T. Rowe Price study.

Dr. Harlow states that the best way to protect oneself from such risk is to limit overall equity exposure to between 5 percent and 25 percent of one's portfolio.[72] This conservative allocation is a much lower number than what many financial gurus would suggest. What's even more amazing about this low percentage is its source. Dr. Harlow is the director of research at the Putnam Institute. Putnam also sells stock and bond mutual funds.

So, how much money should a retiree invest in the stock market? That depends on many factors. For example, I've included a Sleep Factor Quiz in Appendix A. I encourage you to spend a few minutes taking it. It's a tool you can use to determine how much risk you should take with your portfolio.

Remember, when designing financial plans, it is vitally important to ensure, first and foremost, that your income needs are met.

rimm Facts

Forty-six percent of women worry about becoming a bag lady.[73]

Women's worry is well placed. They are well aware of risks and are concerned about the right things. They'll likely live longer than men, yet have less retirement income. (According to the Women's Institute for a Secure Retirement, women's median retirement income is only 58 percent of men's). On average, a newly widowed woman's income decreases by 50 percent, yet her expenses only decrease 20 percent, according to LIMRA. In addition to facing cash flow challenges, women often act as caregivers for aging parents, spouses, or loved ones. Since financial advisors have traditionally focused on male spouses, it's no surprise women are anxious about their finances later in life.[74] "Ever after" doesn't always go so happily for them.

THE THREE-LEGGED STOOL

To build a secure income, let's begin by taking a look at the ways retirement income has traditionally been financed. In the past, a solid income plan in retirement was financed through a combination of pensions, Social Security, and personal savings. By relying on these three funding mechanisms, retirees could count on income that would last for the rest of their lives.

Consider the humble three-legged stool. Together, the three legs of the stool support a solid sitting surface. For the past thirty to forty years, the three-legged-stool income plan approach has worked for most retirees. One-third of their income needs were funded by company pensions; one-third was funded by Social Security; and the final third was funded through personal savings.

But how does such a plan work today? Well, that three-legged stool is in jeopardy.

LEG 1: TRADITIONAL PENSIONS

In the past, people worked for one company for their entire careers before retiring and receiving a gold watch and a pension. This isn't our reality today. Today, most people do not stay with the same employers for their entire careers. Of those that do, men are more likely to have a large pension than their female counterparts are. There are several reasons for this discrepancy.

First of all, many women take time out of their careers to raise children. They have fewer years in the workforce and less time with their employers. Of course, this situation is worse for women who have never worked outside the home; they have no pensions at all.

The second reason for a smaller pension is the wage disparity between women and men. Smaller paychecks translate into smaller pension checks.

Finally, many employers have discontinued pension plans altogether. Currently, only about 8 percent of nongovernmental employers offer a traditional pension plan. This number has dropped. In 1980, 60 percent of workers were offered pensions.[75]

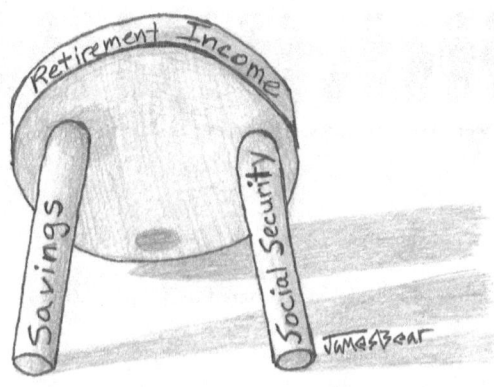

Many retirees do not have pensions, so they depend on personal savings and Social Security for retirement income.

Therefore, Leg 1 of the retirement stool is much smaller than it once was, and for some workers it may not exist at all.

LEG 2: SOCIAL SECURITY

In 1935, when Social Security started, the average life expectancy for women was 63.9 years,[76] and the retirement age was sixty-five. The system was designed with the assumption that most individuals would not collect Social Security, and this income was a "fallback" for those who lived longer lives. Today, due to the miracles of modern medicine, women can now expect to live to be 80.5 years old.[77] Of course, that's just the average. If you're over the age of 65, there's a 50 percent chance you will reach age eighty-six, and a 25 percent chance you will survive to ninety-two.[78] If you take early retirement from

Social Security, there's a one in four chance you will be retired and need income for thirty years.

In 1950, there were 16.5 workers supporting each retiree under Social Security

In 2005, the number of workers plummeted to 3.3 per retiree

By 2025, the number of workers to retirees is expected to be only 2.3

Since 1950 the number of workers supporting each retiree has plummeted and is projected to continue dropping in the future.[79]

The other danger to Social Security is the ratio of workers to retirees has dropped dramatically. As the chart above shows, in 1950, 16.5 workers supported each retiree. By 2005 that number had plummeted to 3.3. By 2025 the number will be only 2.3 workers for each retiree. No wonder Social Security is in trouble.

Although it's impossible to predict what changes will be made to rescue the system, it's likely the future will hold decreases in benefits, increases in retirement age, increased taxation of benefits, or a combination of all three.

Another leg of the stool has shrunk.

THE WIDOW DOUBLE WHAMMY

One of the ugliest surprises of the income puzzle strikes women when they are most vulnerable. I call this the Widow Double Whammy. This is when the comfortable income that many married retirees have enjoyed evaporates when the husband passes away. It can be devastating for the widow.

 Grimm Tale

Fred and Wilma had a traditional marriage and family. Fred worked at the quarry while Wilma had her hands full with Pebbles. After Pebbles had left the cave, Wilma worked part time until that magic day came when the whistle at the quarry blew and Fred slid down the brontosaurus' tail for the last time. "Yabba Dabba Doo!" Their retirement income looked something like this:

Fred's Social Security	=	$1,600
Wilma's Social Security	=	$800
Fred's Pension	=	$1,300
		$3,700

They needed about $3,000 to pay their bills, so Fred and Wilma were able to live comfortably on this income.

Then tragedy struck and Fred passed away. Wilma was left alone. To her shock, she was also left financially alone. Years earlier, when Fred had retired, he had opted for a single-life pension, since it provided a larger income payment than a joint payout did. When he passed away, his pension went away too. This was Wilma's first Whammy.

Wilma had known she would lose Fred's pension when he passed, but had been sure she could manage on their Social Security income.

However, when she went to the Social Security office, she discovered the Double Whammy. The good news was that Wilma was eligible for the larger of the two Social Security payments (hers or Fred's). In this case, she could continue to collect Fred's $1,600 monthly payment. However, she lost her $800 monthly benefit. There is no two-for-one deal with Social Security.

As a widow, Wilma's income looked like this.

Fred's Social Security	=	$0
Wilma's Social Security	=	$1,600
Fred's Pension	=	$0
		$1,600

Fred's passing meant that Wilma's income dropped almost 60 percent. Her comfortable retirement was wiped out with a single stroke. The Widow Double Whammy meant she moved to a new neighborhood: she was forced to live with Pebbles. This wasn't the retirement of which she and Fred had dreamed.

LEG 3: PERSONAL SAVINGS

With the decreasing ability to rely on either employer-funded pensions or Social Security, retirees are going to have to rely more and more on their personal savings to fund their retirement needs.

In the future, many retirees may need to fund the majority of their retirement income with personal savings.

HOW IRENE—AND YOU—CAN BUILD A SOLID HOUSE OF BRICKS

According to a recent report by the U.S. Government Accountability Office, retirees should consider delaying taking their Social Security payments, thus avoiding the possibility that they will run out of money. (Through waiting, the checks will be higher.) The report also recommends retirees purchase annuities.[80] The U.S. government has come to the conclusion that shifting longevity and stock market risk to an insurance company is a good deal for consumers.

While annuities may not be the answer for everyone, in these uncertain times they provide retirees with a kind of safety and stability that cannot be attained through other types of investments. Depending upon how they are structured, these investments can provide lifetime income. Some even come with built-in increases to account for inflation.

However, not all annuities are good. In my opinion, most annuities sold today provide big benefits for the insurance companies and small benefits for the investors. That's why I'm so picky about the accounts I recommend to my clients.

In terms of the optimal plans for generating income, the best annuities are often what I call oxygen-mask plans. When traveling in a plane, you hear, "In case of a decrease in cabin pressure, an oxygen mask will drop in front of you." In addition to living comfortably ourselves, we want to take care of our children—even when they are all grown up—and often want to leave money for them when we pass away.

It's imperative that we take the same approach to legacy planning that we are instructed to take in case of an airplane emergency. As the flight attendant instructs, "Be sure to put on your own mask before helping others." Likewise, you must ensure your income needs are met first. After building a brick (income) house, you can assist your children and grandchildren.

CHAPTER 9

PLAYING "KEEP AWAY" FROM UNCLE SAM

'Twas brillig, and the slithy toves
Did gyre and gimble in the wabe:
All mimsy were the borogoves,
And the mome raths outgrabe.
"Beware the Jabberwock, my son!
The jaws that bite, the claws that catch!
Beware the Jubjub bird, and shun
The frumious Bandersnatch!" [81]

Crazy. Ridiculous. Absurd. Foolish. Ludicrous. Mumbo jumbo.

All of these thoughts may come to mind when we read the poem, "Jabberwocky." I was introduced to this poem in high school, when my class attempted to decipher it during a grammar lesson. The poem introduces plenty of scary creatures—the jabberwock, the bandersnatch, and the jubjub bird—that are ready to attack on sight. This Lewis Carroll poem, originally included in *Through the*

Looking Glass and What Alice Found There, reminds me of another bit of incomprehensible, scary nonsense: the Internal Revenue Code.

The IRS is much like the jabberwock: big, scary, and ready to carry your hard-earned money away.

"Jabberwocky" is a confusing twenty lines long, but it has nothing on the Internal Revenue Code. The Code is 1,500 pages long. The regulations that interpret it consist of six volumes, adding another 10,000 pages to the confusion. If you add in the thousands of IRS revenue rulings, court decisions, and private letter rulings, it's a wonder anyone can make sense of any of it.

It's bad enough that the law is confusing. Few federal institutions have the awesome power of the Internal Revenue Service. The IRS is not benevolent. The institution's job is to collect revenue—out of our pockets. Talk about "the jaws that bite, the claws that catch!" One false move, and your money could be snatched out of your hands.

The jabberwock may be frightening, but I'd rather take my chances with him than with the IRS.

HIGH TAXES?

Most people believe we are currently paying high taxes—too high. After all, Tax Freedom Day arrives later and later each year, according to the Tax Foundation.

In 2011 Tax Freedom Day was April 12.[82] This means the average taxpayer worked 102 days to pay her state, federal, and local tax bills. However, the situation is really much worse. If the IRS actually collected enough revenues to finance the U.S. government's runaway spending spree, Tax Freedom Day would happen on May 23, adding another forty-one days to the calendar. That's almost half the year.

However, believe it or not, even though Tax Freedom Day is coming later and later each year, if you look at historic federal tax rates, we are really paying low taxes. The chart on the next page shows that, compared to past rates, we currently have some of the lowest top marginal federal tax rates in this nation's history.

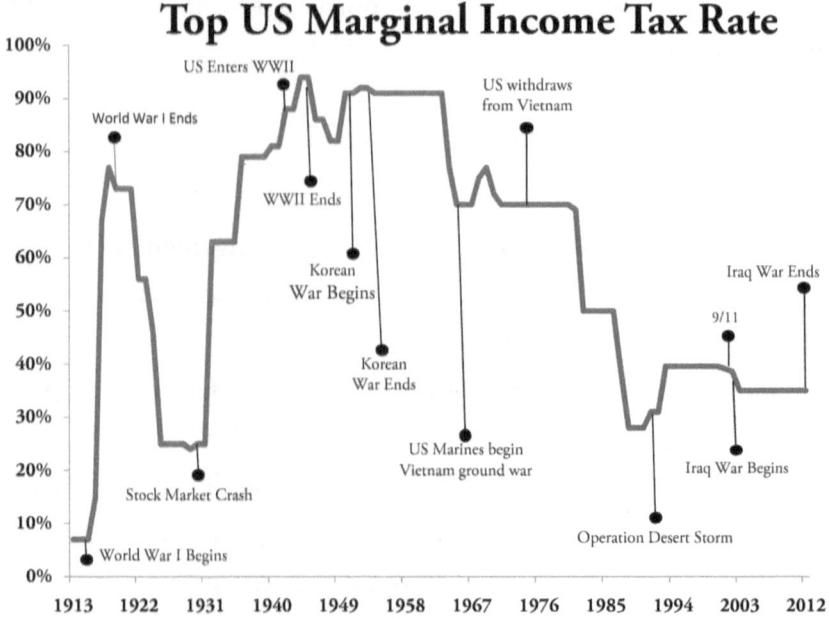

Since the creation of the federal income tax, top tax rates have varied widely. Current rates are scheduled to increase in 2013.[83]

At the end of 2010, Congress and President Obama agreed to extend the Bush tax cuts and keep tax rates low for two more years—until 2013. After that, taxes are scheduled to increase dramatically. When the cuts disappear and the IRS starts to collect the revenues necessary to pay the bills, it may feel as if we won't see Tax Freedom Day until Christmas.

THE FOUR TAX BUCKETS

When investing, it's important to consider the ways that different asset types are taxed. There are four different "tax buckets" in which you can invest your money.

THE TAXABLE BUCKET

The first bucket is the taxable bucket. This is the pay-taxes-now bucket. Taxable accounts are those for which you receive a 1099 form each year and on which you report dividends, interest, and capital gains earned on your investments.

THE TAX-DEFERRED BUCKET

The second bucket is the tax-deferred bucket. This is the pay-me-later bucket. Monies invested in these accounts are not taxed until money is withdrawn from them. They generally fall into two broad categories: qualified and nonqualified plans.

1. Qualified Plans: This first category includes most retirement savings plans sponsored by employers, such as the 401(k), 403(b), and 457 plans; employee stock purchase plans; and profit-sharing plans. These accounts are nicknamed "qualified" plans because, as long as the sponsors agree to follow IRS guidelines, the plans *qualify* for tax-deferred status.

IRA accounts are also considered qualified plans because the institutions that hold the assets agree to follow IRS rules. Most of these accounts allow the employer or employee to take a tax deduction on their returns in the year a contribution is made. To contribute to these plans, you must have earned income. This means you must be working or earning income from a business.

These accounts are great to put money into, but the money can't stay there forever. When you retire, you must begin taking what are called required minimum distributions, starting the year in which you turn seventy and one-half.

2. Nonqualified Plans: This second category includes nonqualified insurance company annuities. Congress has given insurance companies special tax status with respect to the accounts that these companies offer consumers. Such accounts can be great for retirees who are no longer working. Sometimes, these accounts are referred to as unlimited IRAs since there are no annual contribution limits, as there are in qualified accounts. There are also no required minimum distributions in these accounts when the holders turn seventy and one-half.

> **Your Fairy Godvisor Says...**
>
> Careful planning is necessary with both types of accounts in the tax-deferred bucket. At some point, the money will become taxable at ordinary income rates. Often, this can be an ugly surprise!

THE TAX-FREE BUCKET

The third bucket is the best type: it's tax free. There is no tax imposed on earnings held in these three accounts.

1. Municipal Bonds: The tax-free municipal bond (or "muni"), is a very popular investment among high-income taxpayers. The U.S. government, in its effort to assist local governments in raising capital, allows interest paid on most municipal bonds to be exempt from federal income tax.

> **Your Fairy Godvisor Says...**
>
> Use caution when purchasing these bonds. Because of the economic downturn, many local governments are in fiscal trouble. You wouldn't want to invest in a bond just to save money on taxes. If the local government goes broke, your principal is at risk. In addition, a muni is subject to the same interest rate risk that applies to corporate bonds, as discussed in Chapter 5.

2. Roth IRA: The Roth IRA is relatively new type of tax-free investment. Roth IRAs have been around for a little more than ten years. Unlike the contributions to a regular IRA, contributions made to a Roth are not tax-deductible in the year that you make them. However, the growth inside the account is tax-free. Plus, there are no pesky required minimum distributions for you, the account owner.

A recent change in the tax laws now allows for everyone who has an IRA to convert it to a Roth IRA, regardless of income. So, *all* retirees should analyze their existing IRAs and determine if a Roth conversion makes sense for them. This does not mean that every retiree should convert: a conversion is a great opportunity for some, but can be a huge disaster for others. There are hidden tax traps for retirees who do Roth conversions; sometimes, the tax bill is much higher than anticipated. Only by working side by side with a CPA or tax professional can a retiree determine the answer to the question, "To Roth, or not to Roth."

3. Life Insurance: This final tax-free investment, life insurance, has been around for a long time, but has often been underutilized in financial planning. Life insurance companies have been given special breaks for benefits paid to beneficiaries: no tax is due. However, life insurance has changed greatly over the years. These are not your parents' life insurance policies. Retirees who can qualify for life insurance are able to provide their families—and sometimes themselves—with some amazing benefits, and all those benefits are tax-free.

THE TAX-FREE-SQUARED BUCKET

I call this the tax-free-squared bucket because assets held in these types of accounts are not subject to either income tax or estate tax. In 2011 and 2012 estates valued at less than $5 million are exempt from estate tax. Because of this relatively high limit, estate tax is not of concern—now—for many retirees. However, in 2013 the

$5,000,000 exemption drops back to $1,000,000, affecting many middle-class investors.

Because of inflation, being a millionaire is much more common today than it was in 1953, when Betty Grable, Marilyn Monroe, and Lauren Bacall appeared in *How to Marry a Millionaire*. It's unclear how Congress will act regarding estate taxes in the future, but using the tax-free-squared bucket when planning can potentially save your heirs thousands (or millions) of dollars in estate taxes. These accounts include such things as life insurance and charitable trusts set up with attorneys who specialize in estate planning.

HOW IMPORTANT ARE TAXES?

Why is it important to have all of your money in the correct buckets during retirement? Well, to find the answer to that question, we should consider the humble penny.

Benjamin Franklin once said that a penny saved is a penny earned. What if, every day, you could earn a penny for every penny saved? What if we take Franklin literally, and assume that a penny is earned on every penny invested every day for a month? For this illustration, let's assume that on day one, we have one penny. On day two, that one penny doubles, and we have two pennies. On day three, those two pennies double, and we have four pennies. On subsequent days, we have 8 cents, then 16, 32, 64, and so forth.

How much would your single penny grow in thirty-one days? Maybe to $1,000? How about $10,000? Could it be $1,000,000? Believe it or not, the total would be $10,737,418. How does this happen? This increase happens through the power of compound interest, or what Einstein called "the eighth wonder of the world,"[84] exponential growth. That's not bad, for starting out with just a penny.

Of course, this is a pretty unrealistic illustration. There's no investment in the world that will double every day for a month. Not only is this illustration unrealistic from an investment prospective, but it's also unrealistic from a tax perspective. So, to make this illustration a bit more realistic, let's assume the jabberwock at the IRS will be carrying away 28 percent of the earnings every time the account doubles. What would the impact be then?

Believe it or not, when you take out 28 percent of the earnings each time the money doubles, that $10,737,418 plummets to only $116,373.[85] The impact of taxes can cost you more than $10,500,000. That's highway robbery. So, the real power in moving your accounts to tax-deferred or tax-free status is not just the money saved in taxes, but in protecting the potential, exponential growth your money might have.

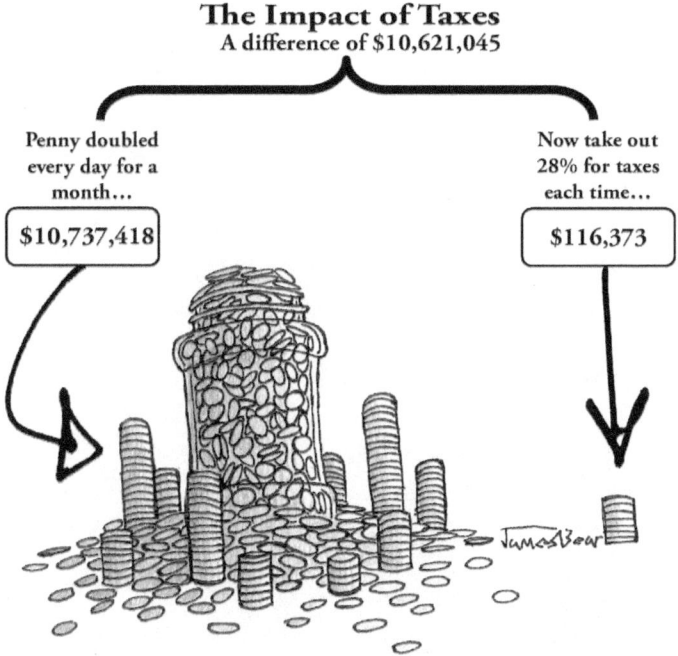

Because of all these factors, it's vitally important to hire an advisor who understands the tax consequences of investments. Otherwise, the jabberwock will carry your hard-earned dollars away to the IRS.

Chapter 10

Building a Solid Legal Foundation

"I want my Mommy."

Okay. I'm a grown-up woman. I'm not throwing a tantrum. But, you know, some days you just want to talk to your mom. You need to feel that unconditional love in her voice as she gently offers her advice. It's on those days that you wish you could return to your happy childhood, when you could crawl into her lap and she would wrap her arms around you and hold you close as you drifted off to sleep.

Today is one of those days. Today is the second worst day of my life. Of course, the worst was the day my mother died. I was devastated. Not only had I lost my mom, but I had also lost my best friend. Now, on the second worst day of my life, I can't even talk to my mom, or confide in her. I've never felt so alone.

It's amazing how quickly things can change from horrible to incredible and back again. Just last night, I met the man of my dreams. For one magical evening, I was transported to a world that I could only fantasize about before. Some people may laugh at the idea of love at first sight, but for us it was real. The time flew so quickly, I didn't realize

> *the magic had come to an end. Now I'm in love with a man who doesn't even know my name. Even worse, I'm back to where I was yesterday morning—at the beck and call of these wicked stepwitches. Why Dad married that woman is a mystery to me. Doesn't he see what a selfish, vain, and petty woman she is? Not to mention her two daughters, who are as mean and spiteful as she is. I wish Mom were here...*

Cinderella is a sad case of estate planning by default. It clearly demonstrates what can happen in the absence of a well-crafted and executed estate plan. Before her story's happy ending, Cinderella was in desperate straits. Treated as a slave by her stepsisters and stepmother after her father remarried, she had obviously received nothing from her mother's estate. All the property went directly to her father and his new family. Cinderella had little control over the disposition of her mother's wealth or personal effects. Even treasured jewelry and heirlooms wound up in the hands of strangers.

Cinderella's life would have become so much better if her mother had made her wishes known before her unexpected passing. The grant of a small legacy would have given Cinderella much-needed freedom and independence. She might have still met her prince, but all her hopes and dreams wouldn't have been placed on a fragile glass slipper.

ESTATE PLANNING ESSENTIALS

Like Cinderella's Mom, you may have avoided making an estate plan, or you may be too busy to make an appointment with an estate-planning attorney and get your affairs in order.

If we make to-do lists, "meeting with an attorney" is not usually at the top of any of them. However, procrastination can have dire consequences. If you don't have a will, the state has one for you—and it may not reflect your wishes.

Instead, proper estate planning allows you to enjoy property during your life and pass on the remaining items at your death to whomever *you choose*. With proper planning, you can ensure that your property is left to intended beneficiaries, not, say, to your husband's next wife.

DOING IT YOURSELF

As tempting as they can be, beware of online "resources." For instance, if you Google "wills," the search result will yield over 82,800,000 articles, websites, and "resources" to review.

A recent search for information on "wills" yielded 82,800,000 online resources.[86]

By the time you finish reviewing all this information, you will be dead—and the state will be dictating your estate plan.

The problem with using the Internet as your primary source for estate planning guidance is finding reliable sources. The websites that pop up first are for companies that have big advertising budgets, but they may not be the best companies for your needs. While you *can* choose to execute a valid will online, beware that you are buying off the rack, so to speak. Online wills are limited in their capacity for customization.

By doing your will yourself, you may be missing out on ideas, strategies, or plans; your documents might not meet state-specific criteria. An excellent estate-planning attorney listens to your story and your family history, and is trained to create a plan that meets your needs. Because of their experience, such attorneys often have suggestions and ideas that might never have occurred to you. This assistance is particularly powerful when your financial advisor, your CPA, and your attorney all join together—as a team—to create your estate plan.

With all those professionals working together on your behalf, documents that meet your needs and goals can be crafted, while you save time, administrative costs, and taxes. These savings could be many times greater than your team's fees.

WHERE THERE'S A WILL, THERE'S A BILL!

Still not convinced you need an attorney? Suppose you go online, or to your local office supply store, and create your own will. What happens when you pass away? In order to transfer assets to your beneficiaries, in most cases your estate must go through probate (the process of transferring assets to beneficiaries). At that point, the court and attorneys will step in. Each year, millions of dollars are spent on probate expenses, including court costs and legal fees. The money you save now can cost your heirs much more later.

One way these costs can be minimized or avoided is by setting up what we call a hope chest trust. Just like a hope chest, you can open the trust's "lid" and put your treasures inside, including your home, bank accounts, and other assets. In addition, as you would with a hope chest, you can remove your treasures whenever you wish.

Many people believe that by placing their assets into trusts that they will lose control and will not be able to manage those assets as they would wish. However, this is not usually the case. If your trust is properly crafted, you will be its trustee during your lifetime: you will be in charge of managing and controlling your trust's assets. During your lifetime, you will have the power to revoke or amend the trust at any time. You can also name a successor trustee who will manage, control, and disburse your assets after your death, or in the event you are unable to act.

ESTATE PLANNING IS NOT ALL ABOUT DYING

While none of us get out of this world alive, estate planning is not just about what happens when people pass away. Most estate plans tend to focus on "death planning": who gets what when the estate holder dies. Yet it's as important to pay attention to "life planning."

For example, what happens if you're in a car accident and can't manage your affairs? If you put a life plan in place, you can designate someone you trust to manage your financial and legal affairs if you become disabled. Additionally, you can have documents created to express your wishes, designating reliable individuals to make medical decisions on your behalf during any period of incapacity (either short-term or permanent). Without these important documents in place, your loved ones, who are responsible for your care, would likely be forced to seek court authorization through a cumbersome guardianship or conservator action.

Your Fairy Godvisor Says...

Life-planning goals can include protecting assets against the high costs of long-term care, which can totally wipe out all the money you've worked so hard to save up. Rely on the team approach: advisors, CPAs, and attorneys can craft a plan to protect your assets, often avoiding the need for expensive, long-term care insurance.

THE TROUBLE WITH GIFTING

Many individuals are so afraid of probate they take drastic steps to avoid it, giving all their assets and property away during their lifetime. While this avoids the expenses of probate and of drafting a trust, such gifting can have unintended consequences.

Let's say Susan gives her house to her son, Mark, with the understanding that Susan will always be able to reside in the home. However, what if Mark dies before Susan, gets divorced, or is in a serious car accident and is sued for everything he owns? Guess what? Susan is homeless. Gifting property allows your children's problems to bump into your problems, and we don't know what the future may hold for our children any more than we know what it will hold for us. The same potential problems arise when adding a child's name to a house title or to a bank or other financial account.

There may also be unfavorable tax consequences for gifting plans. Tax rules regarding gifts are not as favorable as those in place for inherited property. In the above instance, let's assume that Susan gifted Mark her home during her lifetime and nothing bad happened while she was alive. Susan had purchased the home many years previously for $100,000; when she passes away, the home is worth $200,000. Mark is doing fine financially and already has his own home, so he sells Susan's home. At today's 15 percent capital gains rates, he would have to pay $15,000 to the IRS. Here's how the calculation works:

Value at Susan's death	$200,000
Susan's purchase price	$100,000
Capital gain	$100,000
Capital gains tax rate	15%
Tax to IRS	$15,000

Let's compare this with the tax consequences to Mark if he inherits the property:

Value at Susan's death	$200,000
Step-Up in basis	$200,000
Capital Gain	0
Capital gains tax rate	15%
Tax to IRS	0

Why is the number so different? In the case of inherited property, the house would receive what's called a step-up in basis on the day that Susan passed away, and Mark wouldn't have to pay any federal income tax on the gain. If you were in Susan's shoes, would you rather have that $15,000 in Mark's pocket, or in the hands of the IRS?

THE PRINCESS DIANA PROBLEM

Princess Diana married her prince, but she didn't live happily ever after. One of the greatest financial and emotional stress periods in any lifetime comes during a divorce proceeding. In such a situation, not only will you need good legal advice and counsel, but you may also need the services of a financial advisor.

Your financial advisor will help you evaluate your assets, create a budget, and develop financial strategies that will help you make sound decisions and move forward confidently. A financial advisor can also analyze your lifestyle and your assets' longevity, so you and your attorney can seek the most equitable settlement possible.

Both your lawyer and financial advisor should be willing to give you candid advice throughout the divorce process. It may not be what you want to hear, but what is best for your financial future. At a time when you might tend to make emotional decisions, their input is critical. For example, you may have an attachment to the house your children grew up in and want to keep that asset in the settlement, but taking that course of action might have detrimental financial consequences that could affect you far into the future. A good flow of communication between you, your financial advisor, CPA, and attorney is vital to obtaining the best settlement possible.

Unfortunately, many women are poorly equipped to handle financial matters when their marriages dissolve, and fear running out of money. The assistance of a financial advisor, who will help conserve assets and maximize returns on any settlement, and the guidance of a lawyer, who will help tie up any legal loose ends, will facilitate your plans as you move forward.

I HATE ATTORNEYS

It's easy to avoid visiting an attorney because of the sometimes-negative perceptions we develop seeing TV ads for attorneys who will "take care of your DUI" or are "ambulance chasers." We often think of them as predators, scary creatures that can hurt us.

Yet, believe it or not, there are lots of good attorneys out there. The best estate-planning attorneys are not like the scavenger hyenas in *The Lion King*.[87] Instead, they are more like Simba's two guardians, Timon and Pumba.

As women, it is likely we will spend many years living solo: we marry late, live longer, and often find ourselves in periods of transition, when marriages fail or companions pass away. Having legal and financial houses in order is a key component to long-term success and financial well-being. A good lawyer and financial advisor should always be part of your team, not just assistance you seek out in the midst of a crisis.

Cinderella inherited her mother's procrastination gene. After all, she lost track of time and had to rush out of the ball before revealing her true identity to the prince. Only her shoe size saved her. It might be time to move that attorney's appointment to the top of your to-do list.

CHAPTER 11

Finding a "Real Advisor"

Once Upon a Time...

As the girl trudged into the dining room for breakfast, the king, the prince, and the queen were shocked by her appearance. Her bloodshot eyes said it all. It looked as though she had applied grey eye shadow below her eyes to create the dark shadows. Her eyelids drooped so much they seemed to sink into her face. Instead of displaying a healthy, rosy complexion, her skin color was pale and sallow. Even her hair looked dull and lifeless. The royal family couldn't believe she could look any worse than she had the previous night—and that had been pretty bad!

The previous night, when she had arrived on the castle doorstep, dripping wet from the rainstorm, she had looked a bit like a drowned rat. However, after a hot bath and a fresh change of clothes, everyone could see she was a very pretty woman—and the prince was especially enamored. She had something special, something unique. The prince started hoping she was "the one." However, he had been disappointed before. The search for a real princess had been long and difficult. His parents meant the best for him, but he was beginning to give up. They were so darn picky!

Looking at the girl now, the eager prince abandoned all hope. No way would his parents give the thumbs up to this young lady. She looked exhausted, more like a hag than a princess.

The stunned silence was finally broken when the visitor irritably asked, "What did you stuff my mattress with—jousting equipment?"[88]

Upon hearing this question, the queen turned white as a sheet. The girl had passed the sensitivity test. The prince had found his princess. She was indeed the "real" princess they had sought.

The search for a "real advisor" can sometimes feel as daunting as the search for a real princess in a fairy tale. Where do you look? How do you know when you have found "the one"?

FINDING A "REAL ADVISOR"

In the case of the advisor, you want to ensure you are working with an accomplished, experienced professional. Here's a good list of questions to ask a potential advisor.

EIGHT GREAT THINGS TO ASK FIRST

1. What are your professional credentials? How did you get them?

In their search for a real princess, the king and queen wanted to ensure their son's bride was a pure-blooded royal. They knew "title buying" is a too-common occurrence among the aristocracy. In fact, on the website RegalTitles.com, as advertised, people can "Become a lord, lady, duke, countess or the royal title of your choice … in less than a week!"[89]

Regrettably, in the world of financial services, title buying is often commonplace too. For instance, anyone can earn the title, certified senior advisor, by taking a three-and-a-half-day class and writing a check to the sponsoring organization. Contrast this with the title of CERTIFIED FINANCIAL PLANNER™, or CFP®. When you hire a CFP®, you are assured of an advisor who has passed the CFP® Board's rigorous admission and monitoring criteria, which are as follows:

» **Education:** Instead of taking a three-and-a-half-day class, a CFP® must complete the comprehensive curriculum at a college or university approved by the CFP® Board. Alternatively, some advisors fulfill the education requirements through previously obtained professional designations, such as being attorneys or CPAs.

» **Exam:** This two-and-a-half-day exam tests the potential advisor's abilities to apply financial planning knowledge to real-life situations. The exam covers all aspects of financial planning, including tax, insurance, and retirement planning.

» **Experience:** Financial professionals must have several years of experience in financial planning before earning the right to become a CFP®.

» **Ethics:** CFP® professionals are held to the highest of standards in ethics and professional responsibility. They are obliged to uphold principles of integrity, objectivity, competence, fairness, confidentiality, professionalism, and diligence, as outlined in the CFP® Board's Code of Ethics.

» **Enforcement:** The CFP® Board's rigorous enforcement of its Standards of Professional Conduct—which includes releasing disciplinary information to the public—distinguishes CFP® certification from the many other designations in the financial services industry. Every person who seeks CFP® certification is subject to a background check. After attaining certification, any CFP® professional who violates the CFP® Board's ethical or practical standards becomes subject to disciplinary action.[90]

To find out more about the financial planning process, check out the CFP® website, www.CFP.net. The website can also help you locate a CERTIFIED FINANCIAL PLANNER™ near you.

2. How do you invest in your professional education?

This is a great way to find out if your advisor is committed to staying up-to-date on new laws and tax code changes and seeking cutting-edge strategies for helping you preserve and protect your wealth. The best advisors often travel the country several times a year to learn how best to serve their clients (through coaching groups, workshops, and conventions). If your advisor is racking up frequent flyer miles on training trips, that's a good thing.

3. Are you a fiduciary?

As discussed in Chapter 3, make sure your advisor is on the same side of the table as you are. If she has a legal obligation to pledge her allegiance to you—not her firm—you may save yourself some future heartache. You can determine this by checking her licenses. A Series 65 investment advisor representative, for example, has a fiduciary duty to her clients. To investigate these professionals further, check out the website of the Securities and Exchange Commission (SEC) at www.adviserinfo.sec.gov.

4. Can you help me—and my heirs—avoid paying too much in taxes?

Taxes can take a huge bite out of your investment returns, and tax planning must be an integral part of any financial planning process. If your advisor is not a CPA herself, she should be working closely with your CPA or tax advisor to devise investment strategies that legally minimize the taxes paid to Uncle Sam. Remember, tax planning is not done on April 15. Instead, tax minimization strategies need to be in place in advance of tax time for your financial planning to be most effective.

5. What are the "strings" attached to your investment recommendations?

If it sounds too good to be true, it probably is. As discussed in Chapter 7, short of finding a genie in a bottle, there is *no such thing* as a perfect investment. There are positives and negatives to every investment. The good news is that by learning about the negatives, you can make informed decisions and will feel both comfortable with and confident about your investment choices. If your advisor isn't straightforward about investment risks as well as rewards, then *find another advisor—immediately.*

6. Have you written any books on this subject?

Professionals who choose to write have a passion for what they do. They've also taken the time to explain their beliefs and spell out their planning methods. It's not easy to write a book, so by doing so, they demonstrate that they are dedicated to their profession and proud of what they do. Plus, you can read their book and check that the advice they are giving you is in line with their published message.

7. Will you meet with my family members?

A good advisor is not afraid of a client's children, spouse, or significant other. If your daughter is a lawyer and your son a CPA, you are wise to seek their counsel regarding your investments. Don't hesitate to bring all of your family's decision-makers to meet your advisory team. If you all feel the advice given was in line with the advisor's published message, and you all have peace of mind at the meeting's conclusion, then you've created a great team.

8. Are you sensitive to my needs?

Obviously, this isn't so much a question to ask the advisor as it is one to ask yourself. Deep down in your soul, does this person really "get" you? Does she truly understand what your needs are? Does she understand your values? After checking out the more subjective qualifications listed above, let your intuition or gut feelings take over. You may not be able to place a pea under the advisor's mattress, but your gut can tell if the advisor passes your sensitivity test. No matter what an advisor brings to the table in the way of credentials and degrees, the most important degree is the degree of care she takes with her clients.

> ## Your Fairy Godvisor Warns...
>
> This book should not be interpreted as encouragement for you to do all of this yourself. Let's be blunt. You may be the greatest doctor, lawyer, teacher, or accountant your town has ever seen. However, these skills in no way transfer into investment superpowers, and you will not become the next Warren Buffett just by reading a few paragraphs of a book. There is nothing worse than jeopardizing your happily ever after through ideas picked up from a book or online course. That said, smart money management does require you play an active role in your own investments. (You've started doing that already, just by reading this book.) Just don't let your pride get in the way of your common sense. Instead, get help from experienced professionals. Ultimately, it is your responsibility to articulate your needs clearly and question all investments, insurance, and savings products selected by your advisor, ensuring they are in line with your stated retirement and estate planning goals.

Throughout this book, I have attempted to do the impossible: to teach sometimes confusing, complicated, and boring financial concepts and strategies in an entertaining, lively, and fun fashion. I'm guessing that since you've made it to the end, it hasn't been too dull unless you're one of those folks who read the last page first—I won't tell. However, don't think that my lighthearted writing style means that, as a professional, I take financial planning lightly. The subject is incredibly important.

Every woman is unique and may have a wildly personal vision of her ideal retirement. Some ladies want to travel and see the world. Others pursue hobbies and interests closer to home. Spending time with family, especially grandchildren, and friends brings great joy to many retirees. Still others want to leave a lasting legacy for a beloved charity. In today's world, these dreams don't become reality without money. I've seen, all too often, the devastating consequences that can occur with poor financial planning. When you're out of money, you are out of options.

Women today are smart, capable, and intelligent. We don't need handsome princes to survive and thrive in today's world—although if you have one, that's fantastic. It is my dream that every woman is able to retire happily ever after.

Appendix A

DETERMINING YOUR SLEEP FACTOR

In life we take many risks. There are physical risks to our health and well-being that we take the moment we step out of bed every day. There are emotional risks embedded in our relationships with family and friends, and there are financial risks that we take with our money.

When making long-term financial decisions, it's important you match your risk tolerance to your investment strategies. The unofficial name for this matching is your "sleep factor." Sleeping well at night is a basic human need. Studies show that sleep deprivation leads to accidents, sickness, weight gain—or loss—and a host of psychological and physiological problems. Lack of sleep also leads to poor decision making. If you are losing sleep due to the riskiness of your investments, it might be time to reassess your risk tolerance.

For instance, even though Lucy had a very low risk tolerance, she had a large percentage of investments in the stock market. When the market went down, she lost sleep at night, worrying about how the losses would affect her future. When the market went way down, she sold her stock—at the bottom. Lucy is only human. If she had had better knowledge of what her risk tolerance was, she would have been able to determine appropriate investment strategies before she lost money—and sleep.

Knowledge is power.

So, let's begin …

Check the box that best describes how you feel about the following thirteen questions.

1. If you had to rank yourself on a scale of one to five, where do you rate yourself in terms of the risk you are willing to take with your investments? (At the end of the quiz, you'll discover if there is a mismatch between where you are and where you think you are.)
- ☐ 1. Conservative: 0 points
- ☐ 2. Moderately conservative: 2 points
- ☐ 3. Moderate: 4 points
- ☐ 4. Moderately aggressive: 6 points
- ☐ 5. Aggressive: 8 points

2. What is your expectation of annual investment returns, relative to inflation?
- ☐ 1. I'm satisfied with investments keeping pace with inflation: 0 points
- ☐ 2. I like investments to outpace inflation moderately and am willing to accept some long-term risks to achieve this goal: 2 points
- ☐ 3. I prefer investments to outpace inflation significantly and am willing to accept moderate long-term risks to achieve this goal: 4 points
- ☐ 4. I want investments to achieve the highest performance possible and am willing to accept substantial long-term risks to achieve this goal: 6 points

APPENDIX A

3. How strongly do you agree or disagree with the following statement? "I am willing to lose larger sums of money in the short term if I can enjoy potentially higher returns in the long term."
   - ☐ 1. Strongly agree: 8 points
   - ☐ 2. Agree: 6 points
   - ☐ 3. Disagree: 1 point
   - ☐ 4. Strongly disagree: 0 points

4. Investment decisions involve a trade-off between risk and return. Risk is any possibility of loss to your portfolio. Return is the profit on an investment. Generally, investments with the highest potential for gains carry the greatest risk of losses. Let's assume you invested $100,000 and committed to holding that investment for five years. In the examples below, Portfolio 1 is the most aggressive. With this investment, you could lose half of your money over the five-year period, but you have the possibility of tripling your initial investment. In contrast, Portfolio 4 is the least aggressive. In this portfolio, you wouldn't lose your principal and would have some guaranteed return on your investment. Portfolios 2 and 3 are in the middle. Which hypothetical portfolio are you most comfortable with?
   - ☐ 1. Portfolio 1: $50,000 (worst case) or $300,000 (best case): 6 points
   - ☐ 2. Portfolio 2: $75,000 (worst case) or $250,000 (best case): 4 points
   - ☐ 3. Portfolio 3: $100,000 (worst case) or $200,000 (best case): 2 points
   - ☐ 4. Portfolio 4: $110,000 (worst case) or $150,000 (best case): 0 points

5. Which is your investment priority?
   - ☐ 1. Increasing returns: 6 points
   - ☐ 2. Primarily increasing returns while also reducing risk: 3 points
   - ☐ 3. Primarily reducing risk while also increasing returns: 2 points
   - ☐ 4. Reducing risk: 1 point

6. Historically, markets have experienced downturns, both short-term and prolonged, followed by recoveries. Suppose you owned a well-diversified portfolio that fell by 20 percent (for example, your $100,000 initial investment would fall to $80,000) over a short period. Assuming you still have ten years until you begin withdrawals, how would you react?
   - ☐ 1. I would not change my portfolio: 6 points
   - ☐ 2. I would wait at least one year before changing to more conservative options: 4 points
   - ☐ 3. I would wait at least three months before changing to more conservative options: 2 points
   - ☐ 4. I would immediately change to more conservative options: 0 points

7. Which of the following statements best describes your attitude toward long-term investing?
   - ☐ 1. I am willing to accept the lower returns associated with conservative investments that have minimal chance for loss of principal: 1 point
   - ☐ 2. In order to pursue moderate returns, I am willing to accept moderate fluctuations in the value of my investments: 3 points

☐ 3. In order to pursue moderately high returns, I am willing to accept significant fluctuations in the value of my investments: 5 points

☐ 4. In seeking maximum returns, I am willing to accept large fluctuations in the value of my investments and substantial risk of loss of principal: 8 points

8. Investments generate returns in different ways. Which of the following more closely describes your needs?

☐ 1. Dividend yields and interest are better suited for meeting living expenses: 1 point

☐ 2. Overall return is my primary concern; it doesn't matter where it comes from or how it is employed to meet any cash flow needs I may have: 4 points

9. Describe the kind of risk with which you are comfortable:

☐ 1. I could handle being down over a three-year period, but not longer: 5 points

☐ 2. I could handle a one-year loss, but don't want to pursue a strategy that could result in longer periods of loss: 3 points

☐ 3. I could handle losses over one or two quarters, but would not be comfortable subjecting myself to longer down periods: 2 points

☐ 4. I don't want to lose any money, ever. I could only handle a very small loss over a few months at most: 1 point

☐ 5. I could accept being down for longer than three years if my long-term return potential was above average: 7 points

10. When do you expect to begin withdrawing money from your investments?
    - ☐ 1. Less than one year: 1 point
    - ☐ 2. One to three years: 3 points
    - ☐ 3. Four to six years: 5 points
    - ☐ 4. Seven to ten years: 7 points
    - ☐ 5. More than ten years: 10 points

11. For how many years will you be making the withdrawals?
    - ☐ 1. One to three years: 1 point
    - ☐ 2. Four to six years: 3 points
    - ☐ 3. Seven to ten years: 5 points
    - ☐ 4. More than ten years: 8 points
    - ☐ 5. I plan to take a lump sum distribution: 0 points

12. How much do you rely on income from your investments?
    - ☐ 1. Heavily: 0 points
    - ☐ 2. Moderately: 2 points
    - ☐ 3. Somewhat: 4 points
    - ☐ 4. Not at all: 8 points

13. What is your primary investment objective?
    - ☐ 1. Receive current income: 1 point
    - ☐ 2. Invest for future retirement: 3 points
    - ☐ 3. Growth and income: 3 points
    - ☐ 4. Finance an education: 2 points
    - ☐ 5. Accumulate wealth: 4 points

APPENDIX A

ARE YOU READY TO FIND OUT YOUR SLEEP FACTOR?

Add up the total points here _____.
Your total points will determine your individual risk tolerance.

If you scored between *1 and 22*, you are a **Conservative** investor. Safety is important to you, and you should limit the amount you hold in risky investments. Stock market fluctuations make you crazy. Many investors in this category have no investments in the stock market at all. Bank CDs are your favorite places to put your money. Your biggest money risk is inflation. You need to ensure your investments keep up with the cost of living, at least. Otherwise, you will lose money slowly.

If your score was between *23 and 34*, you are a **Moderately Conservative** investor. You want a large portion of your investments to remain safe from market losses but may be able to withstand some ups and downs in exchange for a slightly higher potential return. Conservative investors who invest in the market need to understand that the market generally goes down faster than it goes up. They are most vulnerable to selling at the bottom.

If your score was between *35 and 50*, you are a **Moderate** investor. Generally, you can sleep when the market goes down, even though you don't like it very much. You should strive to create a balance between risk and safety and between growth and income. Your biggest investment challenge is comparing your portfolio to benchmarks.

If you have a balanced portfolio, when the market goes down and your investment is protected from the worst of the downturn, you are happy. However, when the market goes up and your return is not as high, you may feel as though you have failed. Remember the goal of a moderate investor is to smooth out the bumps in the road. Be sure and pat yourself on the back for protecting your investment when the market goes down—and don't worry about keeping up with the Joneses when the market goes up.

If your score was between *51 and 60*, you are a **Moderately Aggressive** investor. You are more likely to gamble with your money. You are comfortable with volatility and aren't depending upon income from investments to meet your living expenses. Typically, moderately aggressive investors have a long-term timeline. If you are one of these investors, you need to make sure you have adequate funds in safe investments for short-term needs, emergency funds, and provision of necessary current income.

If your score was *greater than 60*, you are an **Aggressive** investor. "Pedal to the metal" is the best description for you. You are a gambler with your money. You can avoid the temptation to sell at the bottom, but your biggest risk is buying at the top. You are vulnerable to buying into bubbles that burst. Aggressive investors lost huge amounts of money in the dot.com crash and never regained it. These investors are most likely to lose everything searching for the next Microsoft. If you fit this profile, heed the advice of Kenny Rodgers, in his song "The Gambler":

*You got to know when to hold 'em, know when to fold 'em,
Know when to walk away and know when to run.*[91]

I KNOW MY SLEEP FACTOR. NOW WHAT?

Let's compare this process to how we ladies shop for clothes. Men have it so easy. When they buy a pair of pants, they only need to know two numbers: waist and inseam. Their only decision is whether or not they like the color, fabric, and style. They don't even need to try the pants on. They know the pants will fit. It doesn't work that way for women, however. How many times have you bought something without trying it on and had to return it because it didn't fit right? I know I've had to do that on many occasions. Every woman's body is different.

In the same way, every woman's investment needs are different. A great financial advisor realizes that one size doesn't fit all in investments any more than it does in clothing.

A great financial advisor treats her clients as Sarah Burton treated Kate Middleton when she designed the future Duchess of Cambridge's wedding gown. Burton started with Middleton's measurements (a science) and then designed a beautiful gown, perfect for the royal bride. Any designer could have created a dress that fit Middleton's body. However, delivering a gown that fit both her personality and the royal occasion took someone special.

Similarly, your financial advisor should be building a portfolio not just based on a number but on your personality and situation. When that is done, the final outcome is a perfect fit.

I hope this quiz has been enlightening and helpful. At my office, we use this quiz as a starting point for determining how to advise clients on investing. However, please remember that this is just a starting point. In our practice, my colleagues and I take these scores into account when we develop financial plans for clients, but that is the scientific part of investing. I believe that helping clients is both an art and a science. The art comes in by getting to know each client and customizing a plan to fit her needs.

Appendix B

GLOSSARY

401(k) plan: Section of the Internal Revenue Code that governs plans established by corporations. This plan allows employees to contribute part of their earnings to save for retirement on a tax-advantaged basis. Some employers match part of the employee contributions.

403(b) plan: Similar to a 401(k) plan, this plan is sponsored by public schools, hospitals, and nonprofit organizations for their employees.

457 plan: Similar to a 401(k) plan, except it is sponsored by governmental agencies.

Accountant: Anyone who performs accounting duties as a profession. Accountants may be self-taught or have university educations in accounting or taxation.

Annuity: Fixed payment of money for a period of time (often the annuitant's lifetime). An insurance company typically issues annuity contracts.

Annuitant: Individual upon whose life the annuity is based in an annuity contract.

Asset allocation: Investment strategy in which different classes of assets are held in a portfolio with the objective of minimizing risk.

Bond: Debt obligation in which the issuing entity agrees to pay interest at a stated rate and to repay the loan at a specific future time. Governments and corporations generally issue bonds.

Brokerage firm: Company that acts as an intermediary between the buyer and seller of a security.

CFP® (CERTIFIED FINANCIAL PLANNER™): Regulated by the Certified Financial Planner Board of Standards, Inc., a CFP® is a professional who specializes in providing financial planning services to individuals and business. To become a CFP®, the individual must meet rigorous examination, experience, and ethics requirements. A CFP® is required to act as a fiduciary in all her dealings with clients.

Commodity: In investment terms, a commodity is a class of assets that is considered the same no matter who or what produces it. Commodities include assets that are mined, such as oil, gold, copper, and other precious and semiprecious metals. Agricultural commodities include corn, wheat, sugar, and soybeans. Commodities are traded on exchanges such as the Chicago Board of Trade.

CPA (Certified Public Accountant): Accountant licensed by the state. CPAs must pass the arduous Uniform Certified Public Accountant examination and meet additional requirements defined by the state in which they practice for education, work experience, and codes of ethical behavior.

Deferred annuity: Annuity contract in which the income payments within the contract may be suspended for a period of time. Deferred annuities have tax-advantaged status. Earnings within the account are not taxed until they are withdrawn.

Diversification: Strategy in which multiple assets are owned, primarily for the purpose of decreasing overall risk in a portfolio.

Dow Jones Industrial Average: Commonly referred to as the Dow, this market index is the most closely followed stock index in the United States. Created in 1896, the Dow contains thirty companies.

FDIC (Federal Deposit Insurance Corporation): Independent agency that ensures deposits in member banks. It was created and is backed by the full faith and credit of the U.S. government. Participating banks pay annual premiums to the corporation, which are held in trust to repay depositors in the event of a bank default. Currently, the agency is required to hold reserves of 1.35¢ for every dollar of member deposits. The maximum insurance per individual in each bank is $250,000.

Fiduciary duty: Legal relationship in which the fiduciary is required to place the needs and best interests of the client ahead of her own.

Financial advisor: Generic term used to describe anyone who gives financial advice. No specific qualifications are required to use this title.

Fixed annuity: Contract issued by an insurance company in which the principal and interest payments are guaranteed by the issuing insurance company.

Hedge fund: Private investment fund managed by an investment advisor. Hedge funds often hold a wide array of investments and use a variety of investment strategies. Managers of these funds are given wide discretion as they aim to achieve positive returns on their investment portfolios whether markets are rising or falling. Only institutions and high net worth investors may invest in hedge funds because of strict accreditation rules set by regulators.

Immediate annuity: Investment in which the insurance company agrees to pay fixed income payments during a period of time. The payments may be for a certain number of years (known as "period certain") or the lifetime of the annuitant. In the case of a life annuity, when the annuitant passes away, the annuity payments cease.

Interest: Amount of money paid by the borrower to the lender for the use of money during the term of the loan.

Index: Statistical value of an imaginary portfolio of securities (stocks and bonds) or commodities.

Investment advisor representative (IAR): Person who holds a Series 65 or 66 securities license and represents a registered investment advisor. IARs provide fee-based investment advice to clients. They are held to fiduciary standards in their dealings with clients.

IRA (individual retirement account): Account established to allow for tax-deferred growth for future retirement needs. Generally, contributions to IRAs are tax-deductible when made and are taxed when withdrawn from accounts. Maximum annual contributions are limited to $5,000—$6,000 for account holders more than fifty years old—for employed individuals under the age of seventy and one-half. Certain additional limitations apply to high-income taxpayers.

Liquidity: Funds that can be accessed quickly and without substantial economic penalties. Cash in a checking account is considered a liquid investment.

Mutual fund: A diversified portfolio owned by numerous investors. Professional money managers choose investments for the funds. Mutual funds often specialize in different kinds of investments, for instance, a growth-stock mutual fund or a high-yield bond fund. The amount of risk inherent in a mutual fund varies widely, ranging from low-risk money-market funds to high-risk growth-stock funds.

Nonqualified investment: Account that fails to meet standards for tax-favored status as set forth by the IRS. Generally, investment earnings are taxed each year unless they are held in life insurance or annuity contracts issued by insurance companies.

Probate: Legal process in which assets are transferred to the beneficiary or beneficiaries of a person who has died.

Qualified plan: Retirement account in which investment earnings are not taxed when earned but are taxed when withdrawn from the plan. The plans follow rules set forth in the Internal Revenue Code.

These plans include employer-sponsored 401(k), 457, and 403(b) plans as well as IRAs.

Registered investment advisor (RIA): Investment advisor who is registered by her state securities agency or the SEC to give fee-based investment advice to clients. RIAs are held to a fiduciary standard in their dealings with clients.

Roth IRA: Individual retirement account in which earnings within the account may be withdrawn tax-free after the account has been held five years and the owner has reached the age of fifty-nine and one-half. Contributions to a Roth are not tax-deductible and are subject to limitations similar to those of traditional IRAs.

S&P 500® (Standard & Poor's) Index: Index created in 1957 by Standard & Poor's that includes 500 large company stocks. This index is considered to be the bellwether of the U.S. economy.

Series 7: see Stockbroker.

Series 65 and 66 license: see Investment advisor representative.

Stock: Security that conveys partial ownership in a corporation. The owner of the stock (the stockholder) receives the right to claim a portion of the company's income and assets.

Stockbroker: Registered representative of a brokerage firm who sells securities (commonly stocks, bonds, variable annuities, and mutual funds) to investors.

Suitability: Standard of care in which a stockbroker determines that an investment is appropriate based on information regarding the customer's investment profile, which "includes, but is not limited to, the customer's age, other investments, financial situation and needs, tax status, investment objectives, investment experience, investment time horizon, liquidity needs, risk tolerance, and any other information the customer may disclose."[92]

Tax-deferred: Investment in which U.S. income tax is not paid on investment earnings when earned but when funds are withdrawn from the account.

Trust: Legal instrument in which the individual who establishes a trust (the grantor) dictates how the assets held in the trust are to be controlled during her lifetime and after death. There are many types of trusts available that meet different planning needs.

Variable annuity: Insurance contract that invests in subaccounts that are similar to mutual funds. The value of the contract varies according to the performance of the subaccounts and can be higher or lower than the initial investment. Regardless of the subaccounts' performance, the contract guarantees a minimum income payment at some point in time or the return of the initial investment upon the annuitant's death.

Will: Instrument that dictates how property is to be distributed upon the death of the will's maker. Assets distributed according to a will are passed through the probate process.

Endnotes

[1] Alexander Pope, "An Essay On Criticism," 1711, http://www.ourcivilisation.com/smartboard/shop/popea/critic.htm#Line201.

[2] Bonnie M. Swanson, "Close the Deal: 7 Steps to Selling Your Small Business," Phoenix Woman, Summer 2008, 24–25.

[3] Bonnie M. Swanson, "Changing Hands: Know When and How to Sell Your Business," Phoenix Woman, Spring 2008, 40–41.

[4] Susan W. Sweetser, "Mining Gems," Fall 2006.

[5] Allianz Life Insurance Company of North America, "The Allianz Women, Money & Power Study—Phase II," 2008.

[6] Judy Garland, The Wizard of Oz, film, Metro-Goldwyn-Mayer, 1939.

[7] Roald Dahl, *Charlie and the Chocolate Factory* (New York: Alfred A. Knopf, 1964), 95–98.

[8] The National Debt has continued to increase an average of $3.99 billion per day since September 28, 2007. Brillig.com, December 3, 2011, http://brillig.com/debt_clock/.

[9] U.S. National Debt Clock, accessed December 3, 2011, http://www.usdebtclock.org/.

[10] The Bureau of the Public Debt, Historical Debt Outstanding—Annual, http://www.treasurydirect.gov/govt/reports/pd/histdebt/histdebt.htm.

[11] U.S. National Debt Clock, accessed December 3, 2011, http://www.usdebtclock.org/.

[12] U.S. National Debt Clock, accessed December 3, 2011, http://www.usdebtclock.org/.

[13] The Board of Governors of the Federal Reserve System, Price-Adjusted Major Currencies Dollar Index—Monthly Index, accessed September 1, 2011, http://www.federalreserve.gov/releases/h10/summary/indexnc_m.htm.

[14] U.S. National Debt Clock, accessed December 3, 2011, http://www.usdebtclock.org/.

[15] EuroNews, "Chinese Anger Over U.S. Debt," June 8, 2011, http://www.euronews.net/2011/08/06/chinese-anger-over-us-debt.

[16] Dahl, *Charlie and the Chocolate Factory*.

[17] United States Office of Management and Budget, Fiscal Year 2012 Budget of the U.S. Government, February 11, 2011, http://www.gpoaccess.gov/usbudget/fy12/pdf/BUDGET-2012-BUD.pdf.

[18] U.S. National Debt Clock, accessed December 3, 2011, http://www.usdebtclock.org/.

[19] $2,000 invested annually for forty years with an 8 percent return yields an ending balance of $559,562.

[20] Ruth Helman, Craig Copeland, and Jack VanDerhei, "The 2011 Retirement Confidence Survey: Confidence Drops to Record Lows, Reflecting 'the New Normal,'"EBRI Issue Brief, no. 355 (March 2011), http://www.ebri.org/pdf/surveys/rcs/2011/EBRI_03-2011_No355_RCS-11.pdf.

[21] Brad M. Barber and Terrance Odean, "Boys Will Be Boys: Gender, Overconfidence, and Common Stock Investment," November 1998.[journal title or URL is missing; the original journal was Quarterly Journal of Economics, February 2001, 2, no.1, 261–292]

[22] Allianz Life Insurance Company of North America, "The Allianz Women, Money & Power Study," 2006, https://www.allianzlife.com/womenmoneypower/wmppdf/ENT281_FastFacts1.pdf.

[23] $2,000 invested annually for forty years with a 4 percent return yields an ending balance of $197,653.

[24] The Institute for Women's Policy Research, The Gender Wage Gap for 2010, September 2011, http://www.pay-equity.org/index.html.

[25] Social Security Administration, Social Security Is Important to Women, July 2011, http://www.ssa.gov/pressoffice/factsheets/women.htm.

[26] Social Security Administration, Cost-of-Living Adjustment, April 2012, http://www.ssa.gov/cola/facts/index.htm.

[27] The Consumer Federation of America, the Certified Financial Planner Board of Standards, Inc., the Financial Planning Association, the Investment Advisor Association, and the National Association of Personal Financial Advisors, "Without Fiduciary Protections, It's 'Buyer Beware' for Investors," June 15, 2010, http://www.consumerfed.org/elements/www.consumerfed.org/file/Joint_FOF_Press_Release_Conference_Committee.pdf.

ENDNOTES

[28] The Consumer Federation of America, Fund Democracy, the AARP, the Certified Financial Planner Board of Standards, Inc., the Financial Planning Association, the Investment Advisor Association, and the National Association of Personal Financial Advisors, "Letter to the Chairman of the SEC," Framework for Rulemaking under Section 913 (Fiduciary Duty) of the Dodd-Frank Act, File No 4-604, March 28, 2012, https://www.investmentadviser.org/eweb/docs/Publications_News/Comments_and_Statements/Current_Comments_Statements/120328cmnt.pdf.

[29] Bloomberg News, "Charlie Munger Hangs Up His Cult Heroics," July 9, 2011, http://journalstar.com/business/local/charlie-munger-hangs-up-his-cult-heroics/article_9ab679ad-9785-5e33-ae02-c61f5f058fcb.html.

[30] Mark J. Perry, "The Rise and Fall of the Subprime Mortgage Market," Carpe Diem: Professor Mark J. Perry's Blog for Economics and Finance, July 17, 2008, http://mjperry.blogspot.com/2008/07/rise-and-fall-of-subprime-mortgage.html.

[31] Congressional Budget Office, Report on the Troubled Asset Relief Program, March 2011, http://www.cbo.gov/doc.cfm?index=12118.

[32] Ibid.

[33] "Historical ARM Indexes—Monthly Values," 6-Month CD, April 2012, http://mortgage-x.com/x/indexes.asp.

[34] Janna Herron, "National Credit Card Rates for April 19, 2012," Bankrate.com, April 19, 2012, http://www.bankrate.com/finance/news/credit-cards/interest-rates-041912.aspx

[35] Dorothea Lange, *Migrant Mother*, 1936, Photograph.

[36] Chart created from data downloaded from AnalyzeIndices.com, History of the Dow Jones Industrial Average:1900-2007, http://www.analyzeindices.com/dowhistory/djia-100.txt, and Yahoo Finance, Dow Jones Industrial Average (DJI) Historic Prices, http://finance.yahoo.com/q/hp?s= percent5EDJI&a=09&b=1&c=1919&d=11&e=11&f=2011&g=d&z=66&y=20856.

[37] Richard M. Salsman, "The Cause and Consequences of the Great Depression, Part I: What Made the Roaring '20s Roar," The Intellectual Activist (June 2004), 16. ISSN 0730-2355.

[38] Alfred Eisenstaedt, *The Kiss*, August 14, 1945, Photograph.

[39] "Baby Boom Population—U.S. Census Bureau—USA and by State," updated July 1, 2008, accessed May 18, 2009, http://www.boomerslife.org/baby_boom_population_us_census_bureau_by_state.htm.

⁴⁰ "Number of TV Households in America," Television History: The First 75 Years, http://www.tvhistory.tv/Annual_TV_Households_50-78.JPG.

⁴¹ Chart created from data downloaded from AnalyzeIndices.com, History of the Dow Jones Industrial Average:1900-2007, http://www.analyzeindices.com/dowhistory/djia-100.txt, and Yahoo Finance, Dow Jones Industrial Average (DJI) Historic Prices, http://finance.yahoo.com/q/hp?s= percent5EDJI&a=09&b=1&c =1919&d=11&e=11&f=2011&g=d&z=66&y=20856.

⁴² Victor Hugo King, John F. Kennedy and Jacqueline Kennedy in Dallas, November 1963, Photograph.

⁴³ Chart created from data downloaded from AnalyzeIndices.com, History of the Dow Jones Industrial Average:1900-2007, http://www.analyzeindices.com/dowhistory/djia-100.txt, and Yahoo Finance, Dow Jones Industrial Average (DJI) Historic Prices, http://finance.yahoo.com/q/hp?s= percent5EDJI&a=09&b=1&c =1919&d=11&e=11&f=2011&g=d&z=66&y=20856.

⁴⁴ Chart created from data downloaded from AnalyzeIndices.com, History of the Dow Jones Industrial Average:1900-2007, http://www.analyzeindices.com/dowhistory/djia-100.txt, and Yahoo Finance, Dow Jones Industrial Average (DJI) Historic Prices, http://finance.yahoo.com/q/hp?s= percent5EDJI&a=09&b=1&c =1919&d=11&e=11&f=2011&g=d&z=66&y=20856.

⁴⁵ Chart created from data downloaded from AnalyzeIndices.com, History of the Dow Jones Industrial Average:1900-2007, http://www.analyzeindices.com/dowhistory/djia-100.txt, and Yahoo Finance, Dow Jones Industrial Average (DJI) Historic Prices, http://finance.yahoo.com/q/hp?s= percent5EDJI&a=09&b=1&c =1919&d=11&e=11&f=2011&g=d&z=66&y=20856.

⁴⁶ J.K. Rowling, *Harry Potter and the Sorcerer's Stone* (New York, Scholastic, 1997), 103–104.

⁴⁷ Dalbar, Inc., "2011 Quantitative Analysis of Investor Behavior," (March 2011), 4.

⁴⁸ Wharton Financial Institutions Center, "Real World Index Annuity Returns," March 4, 2010, http://fic.wharton.upenn.edu/fic/policy percent20page/Real-WorldReturns-revisedFIC.pdf.

⁴⁹ Indexes used are as follows. Stocks: S&P 500® (Standard & Poor's) Index; Bonds: Barclays Aggregate Bond Index; Oil: WTI Index; Gold: USD/troy oz.; Foreign Stocks: MSCI EAFE; Homes: Median sales price of existing single-family homes; Inflation: CPI. Average asset allocation investor return is based on Dalbar, Inc., "2011 Quantitative Analysis of Investor Behavior," (March 2011), 3–4.

[50] Dalbar, Inc., "2011 Quantitative Analysis of Investor Behavior," (March 2011), 4.

[51] "Average stock investor, average bond investor and average asset allocation investor performance results are calculated using data supplied by the Investment Company Institute. Investor returns are represented by the change in total mutual fund assets after excluding sales, redemptions and exchanges. This method of calculation captures realized and unrealized capital gains, dividends, interest, trading costs, sales charges, fees, expenses and any other costs. After calculating investor returns in dollar terms, two percentages are calculated for the period examined: total investor return rate and annualized investor return rate. Total return rate is determined by calculating the investor return dollars as a percentage of the net of the sales, redemptions and exchanges for each period." (Dalbar, Inc., "2011 Quantitative Analysis of Investor Behavior," [March 2011], 2.)

[52] Dalbar, Inc., "2011 Quantitative Analysis of Investor Behavior," (March 2011), 3.

[53] Allianz Life Insurance Company of North America, "The Allianz Reclaiming the Future Study," 2010, https://www.allianzlife.com/Variable/content/public/Literature/Documents/ENT-991.pdf.

[54] Annuitization is based on current rates in effect on December 12, 2011. Rates and benefits are subject to change at any time.

[55] Suze Orman, *The Road to Wealth: A Comprehensive Guide to Your Money—Everything You Need to Know In Good and Bad Times* (New York: Riverhead Books, 2008), 510.

[56] James W. Watkins, III, "Variable Annuities," Reading Between the Marketing Lines, 2002, http://investsense.com/variable-annuities/.

[57] Suze Orman, *The Road to Wealth*, 513.

[58] Ibid., 511.

[59] The company that eventually became Bank of America acquired the Arizona Bank in 1986. The CD is fictional, based on current market interest rates available at that time.

[60] Interest rates for this chart were obtained from the following two websites: http://mortgage-x.com/general/indexes/codi_history.asp, and http://mortgage-x.com/x/indexes.asp.

[61] The FDIC, "Designated Reserve Ratio," April 2012, http://www.fdic.gov/deposit/insurance/.

[62] Annuities Institute, How Safe Is An Annuity?, April 2012, http://www.annuitiesinstitute.com/how_safe_is_an_annuity.html.

[63] S&P 500® points are rounded for ease of explanation. Past performance is no guarantee of future performance. Certain restrictions and conditions may apply. This example illustrates the Annual Point-to-Point method with Annual Reset Design using the S&P 500® Index with a 100 percent participation rate and a 10 percent cap on index growth. Index caps, participation rates, and spreads may be subject to change. This illustration assumes no withdrawals.

[64] Ibid.

[65] Ibid.

[66] Ibid.

[67] Steven E. Norwitz, ed., "Dismal Decade Offers Cautionary Lessons for Retirees," T. Rowe Price Report, no. 110 (Winter 2011), 16–18, http://individual.troweprice.com/staticFiles/Retail/Shared/PDFs/PriceReports/Winter2011PriceReport.pdf.

[68] Ibid.

[69] Ibid.

[70] This figure assumes a retiree age of sixty-five using FIA with an initial premium bonus of 9 percent and a lifetime income rider payout of 4 percent with a COLA adjustment of 3 percent per year.

[71] W. Van Harlow, "Optimal Asset Allocation in Retirement: A Downside Risk Perspective," Putnam Institute, 7, https://content.putnam.com/literature/pdf/PI001.pdf.

[72] Ibid., 1.

[73] Allianz Life Insurance Company of North America, "The Allianz Women, Money & Power Study," 2006, https://www.allianzlife.com/womenmoneypower/wmppdf/ENT281_FastFacts1.pdf.

[74] The Hartford, "Why Women Worry (SM): New Research from The Hartford and the MIT AgeLab Identifies Inflation, Health, and Longevity as Major Retirement Worries for Women," 2008, http://ir.thehartford.com/releasedetail.cfm?releaseid=323756.

[75] Alicia H. Munnell, Jean-Pierre Aubry, and Dan Muldoon, "The Financial Crisis and Private Defined Benefit Plans," Center for Retirement Research at Boston College, no. 8–18 (November 2008), 2, http://www.uslabormarket.sakura.

ne.jp/topics/08/08112/financial percent20crisis percent20and percent20private percent20db.pdf.

[76] "National Vital Statistics Reports," vol. 52, no. 14 (Feb. 18, 2004), 34, http://sicp.ai.mit.edu/Spring-2004/projects/project3/nvsr52_14.pdf.

[77] The U.S. Census Bureau, "The 2010 Statistical Abstract: Life Expectancy," 2012, http://www.census.gov/compendia/statab/2012/tables/12s0105.pdf.

[78] LIMRA, Retirement Income Reference Book (2009), 71.

[79] Social Security Administration, The 2009 Annual Report of the Board of Trustees of the Federal Old-Age and Survivors Insurance and Federal Disability Insurance Trust Funds (May 12, 2009), 51–52, http://www.ssa.gov/OACT/TR/2009/tr09.pdf.

[80] The U.S. Government Accountability Office, Retirement Income: Ensuring Income Throughout Retirement Requires Difficult Choices (June 7, 2011), 1, http://www.gao.gov/new.items/d11400.pdf.

[81] Lewis Carroll, *Through the Looking-Glass and What Alice Found There* (Waterville, Maine: Thorndike Press, 2003), 27–28.

[82] Tax Foundation, "April 12 Is Tax Freedom Day," accessed April 12, 2011, http://www.taxfoundation.org/news/show/27166.html.

[83] Data to create this chart was derived from the National Taxpayer's Union, History of Federal Individual Income Bottom and Top Bracket Rates, http://www.ntu.org/tax-basics/history-of-federal-individual-1.html#_edn1.

[84] Albert Einstein, "Compound interest is the eighth wonder of the world. He who understands it, earns it … he who doesn't … pays it," http://www.goodreads.com/quotes/show/76863.

[85] Teresa Bear, "Calculation of Penny Doubling for 31 Days," 2012, http://www.rockartcreations.com/images/PennyDoublingCalculation.pdf.

[86] Search of "will" on www.Google.com performed on December 3, 2011.

[87] Dir. Roger Allers, Rob Minkoff, The Lion King, film, Walt Disney Studios Motion Pictures, June 15, 1994.

[88] Dir. Kathleen Marshall, Once Upon a Mattress, film (music: Mary Rodgers; lyrics: Marshall Barer; book: Jay Thompson, Dean Fuller & Marshall Barer), Walt Disney Studios Motion Pictures, 2005.

[89] http://www.regaltitles.com/.

[90] The Certified Financial Board of Standards, Consumer Guide to Financial Planning (2011), 11–12, http://www.cfp.net/downloads/CFPBoard_Consumer_Guide_to_Financial_Planning.pdf.

[91] Kenny Rogers, "The Gambler," The Gambler, album, United Artists, 1978.

[92] "FINRA Rules: 2111. Suitability," FINRA Manual, July 9, 2012, http://finra.complinet.com/en/display/display.html?rbid=2403&record_id=13390&element_id=9859&highlight=2111.

How can you use this book?

MOTIVATE

EDUCATE

THANK

INSPIRE

PROMOTE

CONNECT

Why have a custom version of *She Retired Happily Ever After*?

» Build personal bonds with customers, prospects, employees, donors, and key constituencies

» Develop a long-lasting reminder of your event, milestone, or celebration

» Provide a keepsake that inspires change in behavior and change in lives

» Deliver the ultimate "thank you" gift that remains on coffee tables and bookshelves

» Generate the "wow" factor

Books are thoughtful gifts that provide a genuine sentiment that other promotional items cannot express. They promote employee discussions and interaction, reinforce an event's meaning or location, and they make a lasting impression. Use your book to say "Thank You" and show people that you care.

She Retired Happily Ever After is available in bulk quantities and in customized versions at special discounts for corporate, institutional, and educational purposes. To learn more please contact our Special Sales team at:

1.866.775.1696 • sales@advantageww.com • www.AdvantageSpecialSales.com

www.ingramcontent.com/pod-product-compliance
Lightning Source LLC
Chambersburg PA
CBHW020909180526
45163CB00007B/2673